CityPack
Bangkok

**ANTHONY SATTIN
AND
SYLVIE FRANQUET**

*Sylvie Franquet is a linguist,
has worked as a model and
translator, and writes a
column for the Belgian
newspaper* De Morgen.
*Anthony Sattin is the author of
several books and is a regular
contributor to the* Sunday
Times. *Together they have
written the AA Explorer
Guides to Egypt, Tunisia and
the Greek Islands, AA
CityPack Guides to Brussels
and Bruges, and AA Essential
Guides to Morocco and
Istanbul. They travel often
and have been returning to
Bangkok for many years.*

City-centre
map continues
on inside back
cover

AA Publishing

Contents

About this book

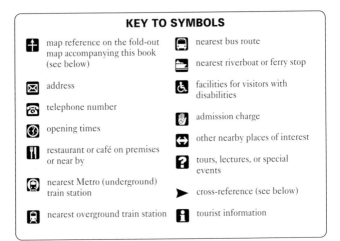

KEY TO SYMBOLS

➕ map reference on the fold-out map accompanying this book (see below)

✉ address

☎ telephone number

◷ opening times

🍴 restaurant or café on premises or near by

🚇 nearest Metro (underground) train station

🚆 nearest overground train station

🚌 nearest bus route

⛴ nearest riverboat or ferry stop

♿ facilities for visitors with disabilities

✋ admission charge

↔ other nearby places of interest

❓ tours, lectures, or special events

► cross-reference (see below)

ℹ tourist information

ORGANISATION

CityPack Bangkok's six sections cover the six most important aspects of your visit to Bangkok.

- Bangkok – the city and its people
- Itineraries, walks and excursions – how to organise your time
- The top 25 sights to visit – arranged from west to east across the city
- Features about different aspects of the city that make it special
- Detailed listings of restaurants, hotels, shops and nightlife
- Practical information

In addition, text boxes provide fascinating extra facts and snippets, highlights of places to visit and invaluable practical advice.

CROSS-REFERENCES

To help you make the most of your visit, cross-references, indicated by ► , show you where to find additional information about a place or subject.

MAPS

- **The fold-out map** in the wallet at the back of the book is a comprehensive street plan of Bangkok. All the map references given in the book refer to this map. For example, the Royal Barge Museum on Soi Rim Klong Bangkok Noi has the following information: ➕ A7 – indicating the grid square of the map in which the Royal Barge Museum will be found.
- **The city-centre maps** found on the inside front and back covers of the book itself are for quick reference. They show the Top 25 Sights, described on pages 24–48, which are clearly plotted by number (**1** – **25**, not page number) from west to east.

PRICES

Where appropriate, an indication of the cost of an establishment is given by **£** signs: **£££** denotes higher prices, **££** denotes average prices, while **£** denotes lower charges.

BANGKOK
life

INTRODUCING BANGKOK

Social problems

Before 1997 there was concern about growing social unrest in Bangkok as the benefits of the economic boom flowed to the management but only trickled down to the labour force. Since the Thai economy crashed in 1997, however, all sectors of the work-force have been made aware that many pre-crash expectations were unreasonable and that social change will come more slowly than predicted.

Floating markets are one of the memorable features of the city

If first impressions were lasting impressions then few people would return to Bangkok: many first-time visitors are horrified by what they find because this is a place that shouts at the senses. Poor air quality, deafening noise pollution, the destruction of old Bangkok, the construction of massive concrete towers to carry a new overland transport system and some of the worst traffic jams in the world (though they are improving) leave many people wondering why they came. Yet despite these and other environmental problems there are ways around the worst of Bangkok, and those who find them will leave with an image of a fascinating, exotic and beautiful city.

Bangkok has experienced the full urban development cycle in two dramatic centuries, growing away from its origins by the water (► 10 and 12) to become a city where new buildings are in such demand that contractors keep work going on their sites 24 hours a day. Bangkok's progress is dynamic and, especially coming from tired old Europe, it is thrilling to see. The drawbacks – most obviously pollution – are something Thais seem prepared to accept as the price of their success. Partly because of the traffic problem, the move away from the waterfront has now turned full cycle: as the city gets ever more crowded, people are returning to work and live by the water, with its fresher air, cooling breezes and improving transport.

While the fast, modern face of the city is changing, and new shops, bars, hotels and restaurants open, old Bangkok is still there to be found in the many beautiful *wats* (temples) and wooden houses, in the life along the river and *klongs* (canals), in the markets and also, still, in people's attitudes. For in spite of their appetite for all things modern and their craving for *sanuk* (fun), Thais are nothing if not conservative, something you will notice in particular during festivals.

Leaving Bangkok helps you stay sane when you live here. The sea is very close (though the further you go from Pak Nam – the 'River Mouth' – the cleaner the water), while places such as the ancient capital of Ayutthaya (a Unesco World Heritage Site) and the River Kwai and its infamous bridge are just a day-trip away.

There is something unique about Bangkok which encourages people to come back again. Partly it's the discovery that this city of 9.4 million is neither the 'City of Angels' that its promoters would like it to be, nor the 'Sin City' that some foreigners dream of finding, though it does contain both of these elements. For most of us the attraction is the strangeness of the colours and light, the shapes of buildings, the sight and smell of market ingredients and the wonderful dishes created from them, and, above all, the character and tradition of the city's people. When you leave them, they'll say *sawasdee* – not only 'goodbye', but also 'hello' again.

Mai pen rai

This expression translates roughly as 'never mind', 'no problem', 'it doesn't matter' and goes together with *jai yen* (literally 'cool heart'), the social imperative that one should not show one's feelings openly. So even if something bothers people, they'll say *mai pen rai*. What they think is, of course, another matter.

View from the Golden Mount, a man-made hill nearly 80m high

A DAY IN THE LIFE OF A THAI

The monk's day

Monks wake early. Up before dawn, they recite morning prayers before leaving on their rounds of the neighbourhood with their alms bowls, into which people put food offerings. The monks rely entirely for their livelihood on the generosity of the community. The life of a monk is guided by 227 moral precepts, and should be one of retreat and contemplation. However, the monkhood has recently been accused of losing touch with the age-old traditions, as many ex-prisoners and drug addicts have joined the Buddhist brotherhood to escape the reality of their lives.

Right: a monk receiving food Opposite: Wat Phra Keo with (inset) a girl at prayer

However early you wake in Bangkok, there will already be cars in the streets and foodstalls serving breakfast. The call to table in Thailand is *khao taow*, 'eat rice', something that is traditionally done three times a day. For breakfast that often means rice soup, though now it may be rice crispies instead. The city's traffic problems have forced businesses to stagger work times, but as most schools start at 8:30AM many people have to leave home hours before. Thais love to laugh, and even at work time will be found for some *sanuk* (fun). Lunch is served in most places between 12 and 2, and for many people will consist of a bowl of rice and stir-fry, noodles or, increasingly, a hamburger from one of the growing number of US-style fast-food restaurants. But wherever they have lunch, Thais don't eat alone (more of that *sanuk* mentality).

The traffic gets jammed again from 3 to 4PM, when schools finish, and after that offices start to close, which means that no one goes anywhere very fast. Between now and early evening, when dinner is eaten, people exercise, some on jogging tracks and others in huge shopping plazas. Dinner is eaten early and, as always, with family or friends. Many working people, who have to wake so early in the morning, will stay at home on weekday evenings.

In summer, it's a treat to get out of the city to the seaside. When they stay in the city Thais like to do something, whether it's flying kites, shopping in Chatuchak Weekend Market or making offerings at temples. Happily, weekend traffic is lighter and so it is easier to get around the city. Thais like to eat out, especially at the weekend. After dinner there are the night markets, cinemas playing mostly macho films, bars and a growing number of nightclubs. Finally, there is the thrill of the unusually fast ride home.

BANGKOK IN FIGURES

THE PLACE

- Bangkok lies 14 degrees north of the Equator, covers an area of 560sq km (the metropolitan area covers 1,565sq km) and is home to more than 400 Buddhist temples (Thailand has 23,700 in all)
- Bangkok's full name is the longest place-name in the world, but is shortened to Krung Thep ('City of Angels')
- Bangkok is 9,525km from London and 8,972km from Frankfurt

THE PEOPLE

- Roughly 16 per cent of all Thais (9.4 million people) live in Bangkok. Some 600,000 foreign tourists visited Bangkok in 1997
- Almost half of Thais are under 30, yet the growth of Thailand's urban population slowed from 5.3 per cent per annum in 1975 to 2.4 per cent in 1997
- Nearly 80 per cent of Thai university graduates live in Bangkok

THE TRAFFIC

- Bangkok's first paved road, Thanon Charoen Krung, or New Road, was laid in 1862
- In 1997 90 road projects were set up in the city in an attempt to reduce the notorious traffic congestion
- At last count (1996) there were 109,000 cars in Bangkok

9

A CHRONOLOGY

1530s King Phrajai (ruled 1534–46) re-routes the Chao Phraya river some 76km south of his capital Ayutthaya (► 20), making possible the creation of Thonburi on the west bank and Bang Makok on the east

1768 After the Burmese destroy Ayutthaya, the previous Thai capital, General Phraya Taksin establishes a new capital at Thonburi, where he is crowned King Boromaraja IV (commonly known as King Taksin). As the Burmese are dragged into a conflict with China, Taksin builds an empire that includes Lanna (northern Thailand), Cambodia and parts of Laos

1782 Taksin is deposed by one of his generals, Thong Duang (the man responsible for bringing the Emerald Buddha back from Laos), who is crowned Rama I. He builds himself a new capital on the site of an old fort called Bang Makok, which he calls Krung Thep ('City of Angels'); we know it as Bangkok

1824 British trader Robert Hunter sees Siamese twins (the first recorded case; ► 34) swimming in the Chao Phraya river

1825 King Rama III (ruled 1824–51) responds to growing European influence by closing the mouth of the Chao Phraya river with a massive iron chain. His isolationist policy doesn't work: the Burney Treaty of 1826 lowers taxes on British goods passing through Bangkok in return for guarantees of Thai sovereignty

1851 Unlike his brother, King Rama IV (ruled 1851–68) encourages change. His vision and political skills ensure that Thailand is the only state in the region to retain independence during the colonial period

1868 Rama V (King Chulalongkorn, ruled 1868–1910) continues social reforms, builds railways, has electricity installed in Bangkok (1884) and encourages closer contacts with the West, but is forced to cede territory in Indo-China

1912 Thailand's first manufacturing business opens. The first military coup is staged, this time an unsuccessful bid to oust the monarchy

1932 King Prajadhipok (Rama VII, ruled 1925–35) celebrates the 150th anniversary of the Chakri Dynasty (▶ 12) in April, but in June a bloodless coup replaces absolute monarchy with a constitutional monarchy and a mixed civil/military government. When the new rulers ignore the constitution, the king abdicates in 1935

1939 The country's name is changed from Siam to Prathet Thai, meaning 'Land of the Thais'

1942 Thailand capitulates to the Japanese, and the Thai leader Phibun Songkhram declares war on the US and Britain. However, the Thai ambassador in Washington, Seni Pramoj, refuses to deliver the declaration; in 1945 he becomes prime minister

1946 Thailand is admitted to the United Nations. King Rama VIII, who has spent most of his life in Europe, arrives in Thailand but is shot soon after. He is succeeded by his brother, HM King Bhumibol Adulyadej (King Rama IX)

1947 Another coup returns the military to power, where they remain until 1973. In the 1960s, the US begins building military bases within Thailand to help with the Vietnam War. The needs of the US military (including 'R&R' facilities) bring huge sums of money into Thailand and change Bangkok for ever

1991 Democratically elected PM Chatichai Choonhavan is ousted in a military coup

1992 Some 50 people die in anti-NPKC (National Peace-Keeping Council) protests. The king forces the resignation of the NPKC leader and new elections are held

1997 The Thai economy crashes and the baht is devalued

11

PEOPLE & EVENTS FROM HISTORY

Rama VI, king between 1910 and 1925

The longest reign

When the national anthem is played (8AM and 6PM daily), people stop and stand to attention. This is not mere lip-service: HM King Bhumibol Adulyadej (Rama IX) is adored in a way that puzzles many foreigners. The king's position of 'revered worship' is assured by the constitution, but he has earned esteem for his able leadership (he defused the explosive situation after the 1992 anti-government protests in Bangkok) and for his public projects.

KING RAMA I

Thong Duang, a *chakri* or military commander in the army of King Taksin, was known as one of Siam's most able leaders. It was he who captured the Emerald Buddha, a statue revered for its great powers of protection. The statue certainly worked well for Thong Duang, for King Taksin was later deposed and the leading figures in the country chose the *chakri* as his successor. On his coronation in 1782 he adopted the name of Ramathibodi, a king of Sukhothai, moved his capital across the river to Bangkok and founded the Chakri Dynasty, which survives to this day. Later, Ramathibodi was known more simply as King Rama I, a practice subsequent Chakri kings have all adopted.

KING RAMA IV

Also known as King Mongkut, Rama IV (1851–68) is an often misunderstood figure, thanks mainly to the way he was represented by the English governess Anna Leonowens, who was employed by the king to educate his children (and, Ms Leonowens insisted, also himself) in the ways of the West. After the king's death, Ms Leonowens published an account of her employer in *The English Governess at the Siamese Court* (1870). Its patronising portrayal of the king is still considered offensive by many Thais, as is the Hollywood film version, *The King and I*, with Yul Brynner as King Mongkut.

KING RAMA V

King Chulalongkorn (Rama V) is credited with keeping Thailand independent in the second half of the 19th century, but he did so at a cost. Although his kingdom was guaranteed by a treaty with Britain, in 1893 France demanded that Thailand hand over Laos. When France attempted force, the Thais resisted and one of the French officers was killed. This provided a pretext for sending gunboats up the Chao Phraya. Unable to protect itself and with Britain refusing to help, Thailand ceded Laos in 1893, Cambodia in 1907 and three Malayan states to British Burma in 1909.

BANGKOK
how to organise your time

ITINERARIES

First-time visitors are often overwhelmed by Bangkok and its notorious traffic problems. You can see the essential sights in four days, but to explore the canals (*klongs*) and the smaller temples (*wats*) you will need more time. The secret is to visit just one area and to use the river for transport where possible to avoid traffic jams.

ITINERARY ONE	**RATTANAKOSIN (ROYAL CITY)**
Morning	Start early in the morning with a visit to the extensive grounds of the Grand Palace (► 29) and Wat Phra Keo (► 30). Walk to the north of the palace grounds to reach the large open space of Sanam Luang, visiting the Lak Muang pillar (► 32) on the way
Afternoon	Stroll around the sides of Sanam Luang and among the market stalls, and have your fortune told. Return along more stalls on Thanon Maha Rat to Wat Po (► 33), and end the afternoon with a relaxing traditional massage
Evening	Take a river cruise with dinner and view the Grand Palace, illuminated at night (► 64)
ITINERARY TWO	**THE RIVER**
Morning	Start early in the morning with an organised boat trip (► 19) to the floating market (► 25), Wat Arun (► 27), the Royal Barge Museum (► 24) and Wat Ra Kang (► 26)

Spirit houses, part of Thai life, are all over the city

Afternoon	Take a public boat into one of the canals to discover a world that is much more rural, and sometimes even jungle-like (➤ 58 and 90). Watch the sunset and have a drink on the terrace of the Oriental Hotel (➤ 39)
Evening	Have dinner at one of the riverside restaurants (➤ 62–5), perhaps taking in a cultural show

ITINERARY THREE
NATIONAL MUSEUM AND CHINATOWN

Morning	A visit to the National Museum (➤ 31) takes about three hours. Catch an express boat to Ratchawong pier to visit Chinatown
Afternoon	After an enjoyable *dim sum* lunch in a Chinese restaurant (➤ 66), stroll around the picturesque and chaotic lanes of Chinatown (➤ 17 and 36). If the traffic is not too bad in the late afternoon, take a taxi to Lumphini Park (➤ 45) and hire a rowing boat on the lake or watch the young couples passing by
Evening	Have dinner in one of the many excellent Thai restaurants around Thanon Silom and Thanon Surawong (➤ 62–3), then take a stroll through Patpong night market (➤ 18) and have a few drinks in one of its many bars

ITINERARY FOUR
SUKHUMWIT

Morning	Vimanmek Palace (➤ 37) and its museums, and Suan Pakkard Palace (➤ 43), both set in peaceful gardens, offer a welcome break from the hectic city
Afternoon	Another oasis is Jim Thompson's House (➤ 41); the rest of the afternoon can be spent in the huge shopping centres on and around Thanon Sukhumwit and Thanon Ploenchit
Evening	Try one of the many good restaurants around Thanon Sukhumwit, then take an evening stroll in Sukhumwit night market (➤ 18) or watch the dancers at the Erawan Shrine (➤ 44)

WALKS

The Buddha at Wat Phra Keo

RATTANAKOSIN (ROYAL CITY)

See where it all began, with the grandest of the city's temples, street markets, a park and the possibility of a relaxing massage on the way.

Start at Maha Rat pier, turning right on Thanon Maha Rat and immediately left on Thanon Sillapakorn. The entrance to one of Bangkok's oldest temple complexes, Wat Mahathat, is on the left, opposite Sanam Luang. Walk across Sanam Luang to the city's shrine, the Lak Muang pillar, more or less opposite the entrance to the Grand Palace. Veer to the right on to Thanon Nophralan and make a left turn on Thanon Maha Rat to stroll through the thriving street markets that sell amulets, fruits and various life-size portraits of the king. Past the palace, on the left-hand side, rise the impressive roofs and *chedis* (pagodas) of Wat Po, where you can relax with a massage.

Walk along Thanon Chethuphon, take a left on busy Thanon Sanam Chai, then turn right into Thanon Sararom. Wat Ratchapradit is on the right and a bizarre sculpture of a pig lies at the end of the street. Cross the canal by the foot-bridge to Thanon Ratchabopit, with yet another temple, Wat Ratchabopit, to the right. Continue along the same road and make a left turn on Thanon Titong, with its local shops. At the intersection with Thanon Bamrung Muang, explore the wonderful Wat Suthat and the nearby Giant Swing. Head along Thanon Din So towards Democracy Monument, built in honour of modern Thai parliamentary monarchy and now a chaotic, traffic-packed roundabout.

For refreshments there are foodstalls on Sanam Luang and near Wat Po, as well as the Kanit Restaurant (➤ 68) near Wat Suthat, serving good French and Italian food, and Vijit for simple Thai food (➤ 63).

THE NARROW LANES OF CHINATOWN

From Ratchawong pier, walk along Thanon Ratchawong and then turn left into Thanon Annuwong. To the right is an old Chinese house. Walk on as far as Thanon Maha Chak. Take a right here and walk for 150m until you see an ornate portal on the left leading to Wat Chakrawat; visit the crocodile pond.

Return to Thanon Maha Chak and turn left, continuing as far as busy Soi Wanit 1 (Sampeng Lane). Turn right here, cross over Thanon Ratchawong and carry straight on, exploring the alleys but always returning to Sampeng Lane as it is easy to get lost. At No 360, turn left into Soi 16, with its amazing variety of food products. Cross Thanon Yaowarat and walk to Thanon Charoen Krung. Cross the road and continue about 30m to the left, past fruit and sweet stalls, to the entrance of the Chinese temple of Leng Noi Yee. The temple is very popular with locals, who make offerings of everything from ducks and fruit to gold leaf and incense. Returning to Soi 16, continue through an even more exotic food market which ends in Chinese funerary supplies shops that sell paper objects to be burned with the dead. At the end of the street turn right into Thanon Phlabphlachi, with shops selling red and gold shrines of all sizes. Turn left on Thanon Charoen Krung (New Road) and follow it as far as the fountain on the square, then turn left into Thanon Traimit to find Wat Traimit on the left.

If the foodstalls found all over Chinatown are too public for you, try the delightful *dim sum* at Siang Ping Loh in the Grand China Princess Hotel (➤ 66) or the S&P restaurant on the 2nd floor, which has cheaper Thai and Chinese dishes.

THE SIGHTS

- Wat Chakrawat
- Soi Wanit 1 (Sampeng Lane; ➤ 36)
- Thanon Yaowarat
- Soi 16
- Leng Noi Yee Temple
- Chinese funerary objects on Soi Isaraphap
- Wat Traimit (➤ 40)

INFORMATION

Distance 2½km
Time 3–4 hours, excluding stops
Start point Ratchawong pier
➕ D10
🚌 A/C bus 1, 7
🚢 Ratchawong pier
End point Wat Traimit
➕ E10
🚌 A/C bus 1, 7

Wat Traimit

EVENING STROLLS

Racy nightlife in Patpong

RED-LIGHT DISTRICT OF PATPONG

Start at the top of Thanon Silom at the corner of Thanon Rama IV, where Thais young and old come for *sanuk* (fun). There are foodstalls on both sides of Thanon Silom, some serving excellent fresh seafood and home-made curries. On the south side of the road are stalls selling imitation brand-name goods such as Cartier and Rolex watches, Tommy and CK shirts, bootleg tapes for next to nothing, and Prada and Gucci bags. At Soi Patpong 1, turn into the very popular night market, with more fakes, Tintin T-shirts and cheap souvenirs, as well as the famous and often seedy go-go bars, with glaring neon lights and young men offering menus of striptease shows. Shop or drink till you drop, or stroll around the lanes off Patpong with the better bars and clubs, watching their often very different clientele. End your stroll on Thanon Surawong or further down Thanon Silom.

SUKHUMWIT NIGHT MARKET

Start at the western end of Thanon Sukhumwit, next to the railway tracks and under the expressway flyover, perhaps after a meal in one of the restaurants on nearby Soi Ruam Ruedi (► 68–9). Hoping to emulate the success of the night market in Chiang Mai in northern Thailand, traders have set up this market in Bangkok, and offer a wide variety of souvenirs, silks and crafts. There is also quite a variety of foodstalls and both girlie and other bars. Walk along the north side of Thanon Sukhumwit towards Soi 5. From here as far as Soi 11 more colourful stalls line the road with cheap goods designed to tempt tourists; never forget that bargaining is an intrinsic part of the game. Just past Soi 11 is the Ambassador Hotel, offering a different sort of night market on its compound and selling a variety of food.

INFORMATION

Patpong
Distance 1km
Time 1 hour or all night
Start point Corner of Thanon Silom and Thanon Rama IV
➕ G11
🚌 A/C bus 2, 4, 5, 15
End point Thanon Surawong or Thanon Silom
➕ G11
🚌 A/C bus 2, 4, 5, 15

Sukhumwit
Distance 1km
Time 1 hour
Start point and end point Beginning of Thanon Sukhumwit
➕ J9
🚌 A/C bus 1, 8, 11, 13

ORGANISED SIGHTSEEING

The Tourism Authority of Thailand ☎ 694 1222 (64 lines); fax 694 1220/694 1221 does not organise tours, but it will provide visitors with information about accredited agents, including those listed below:

SEA Tours ☎ 251 4862–9 (also offices in several hotels) is the American Express representative in Thailand, and offers several half-day guided tours. Those on offer are the Grand Palace, including Wat Phra Keo; city and temples, including Wat Po; an early morning boat tour along canals to the floating market, with a stop at Wat Arun; Jim Thompson's House and Suan Pakkard Palace; and (afternoon) canal tours by long-tail boat and converted rice barge.

Steep stairs up Wat Arun lead to a fine viewpoint

World Travel Service ☎ 233 5900 (also branches in several hotels), Diethelm Travel ☎ 255 9150/9170 (also branch offices) and Turismo Thai ☎ 245 1551/1571 (also branch offices) offer a similar range of tours. All of these agencies can also arrange private tours with guides who speak a variety of languages. Chao Phraya Chartered Co Ltd ☎ 433 5453/435 7699, is a smaller company running daily river/canal trips each afternoon from River City Shopping Complex.

CULTURAL TOURS

Several companies offer night-time cruises that serve Thai food accompanied by Thai classical dance (➤ 64). At the top end of the market is the Oriental Hotel (➤ 39), which runs a Thai Culture Programme each afternoon starting with an introduction to Thai ways, including a canal trip (Monday), a class on Thai religion with a visit to Wat Po (Tuesday) and Thai art with a visit to the National Museum (Friday) ✉ 48 Soi Oriental ☎ 236 0400. For the more adventurous, Amazing Bangkok Cyclists organises mountain bike trips that reveal the city's quiet backstreets and *klongs* ☎ /fax 322 9481.

Special outing

East West Siam (☎ 256 6669; fax 256 7166) runs unusual canal tours which combine exploration of more remote Thonburi canals with insights into Thai ways and culture. Highlights include visits to a traditional Thai teak house for lunch and a cooking lesson, a small temple and a primary school. The tour ends with a visit to the Royal Barge Museum (➤ 24).

EXCURSIONS

INFORMATION

Ayutthaya

Distance 76km north of Bangkok

- 🚌 Hourly buses (journey time 2 hours) from Bangkok's Northern Bus Terminal
- 🚆 Hourly trains (journey time 1½ hours) from Hua Lamphong (1:30PM)
- ❓ The Oriental Hotel (☎ 236 0400) runs guided day-trips by air-conditioned coach and on the *Oriental Queen*. The Shangri-La Hotel (☎ 236 7777) offers a similar service. The Chao Phraya Express Co (☎ 222 5330) sails to Ayutthaya and Bang Pa-In on Sun, leaving 8AM from the Maha Rat pier. The *Mekhala* rice barge and the more luxurious *Manohra Song* allow you to sail overnight and can be booked through Asia Voyages (☎ 256 6153; fax 256 6665)
- ℹ️ TAT Office ✉ Thanon Si Sanphet ☎ 035 246 076/7

Pak Nam

Distance 30km from city centre

Journey time 1½–2 hours

- 🚌 An air-conditioned bus (no 11) runs from Thanon Sukhumwit
- 🚤 Long-tail boats can be rented; be sure to haggle

Topiary at Bang Pa-In, summer palace of Rama V

AYUTTHAYA, BANG PA-IN AND BANG SAI

When Bangkok was a small village, Ayutthaya was Thailand's capital, a glittering city on an artificial island encircled by canals, with scores of palaces, hundreds of temples and more than a million inhabitants. For over 400 years – until 1767 when it was sacked by the Burmese – Ayutthaya was one of the region's great cities. Of the old city – now scattered amongst the buildings of modern Ayutthaya, and designated a World Heritage Site by Unesco – Wat Mahathat, Wat Ratburana and Viharn Phra Mongkol Bopit are not to be missed. In the mid-19th century at nearby Bang Pa-In, the Thai royal family built a country retreat in a variety of architectural styles, including classical Thai, Chinese and Italian, while at Bang Sai, HM Queen Sirikit has helped establish a foundation for crafts, where a good range of handiwork is on sale.

RIVER TRIP TO PAK NAM

A hundred years ago travellers arrived in Thailand at Pak Nam (literally 'River Mouth'), where the Chao Phraya river flows into the Gulf of Thailand. As you travel south by boat from central Bangkok, you will see that the river is soon taken over by business. You cut in front of tugs pulling chains of rice barges and run ahead of them to Klong Doei (Klong Toey), Bangkok's international port, where freighters load the exports of Thailand's booming economy. South of the port the Chao Phraya widens and the banks are crowded with greenery. Pak Nam, where many trawlers tie up, has important fish factories, a renowned *wat* and, near by, an excellent fish restaurant.

The famous bridge spanning the River Kwai

RIVER KWAI

Glorified in David Lean's film *The Bridge on the River Kwai*, the 'Death Railway', as it is known, was built by Allied prisoners of war and Asian labourers in the 1940s with the loss of many lives, and then rebuilt after the war. Kanchanaburi, the town that has grown up beside the bridge, is now a major tourist attraction. Apart from the bridge itself and train rides along the track, the War Museum and the Kanchanaburi War Cemetery, last resting place of 6,982 Allied prisoners of war, attract many visitors. The Chung Kai War Cemetery, 2km south and built on the site of a prison camp, contains the graves of 1,750 of the estimated 16,000 Allied prisoners of war who died during construction of the railway. The JEATH War Museum lies south of the bridge.

HUA HIN

Thailand's first resort, Hua Hin, is still the most pleasant beach within easy reach of Bangkok. The town remained a quiet backwater until recently, but has subsequently undergone some serious tourist development; despite this, it retains a quaint Chinese quarter and lovely fishing harbour. In the early 20th century the Thai royal family recognised Hua Hin's potential and built several villas and palaces here (closed to the public). The famous Railway Hotel, now the Sofitel Central, was built by Prince Purachatra and appeared in the film the *Killing Fields*.

INFORMATION

River Kwai
Distance 130km from Bangkok
Journey time 3 hours

🚌 Regular buses from Bangkok's Southern Bus Terminal

🚆 Two trains daily for Kanchanaburi from Bangkok Noi Railway Station (third class only; no reservations). State Railways of Thailand runs a special tourist train (weekends and holidays), departing 6:35AM from Bangkok's Hua Lamphong Station (☎ 223 3762/225 6964; reservations are essential)

❓ RSP Travel Centre (☎ 251 7552) and other major travel agents offer day-trips

ℹ️ TAT office ✉ Thanon Saengchuto ☎ 034 511 200

Hua Hin
Distance 230km south of Bangkok
Journey time 3 hours

🚌 Regular A/C buses from Bangkok's Southern Bus Terminal

🚆 Regular trains from Hua Lamphong station (3–4 hours)

❓ Also one flight daily from Bangkok

ℹ️ TAT Office ✉ 114 Thanon Phetkasem, Hua Hin ☎ 512 120 🕐 Daily 8:30–4:30

WHAT'S ON

Buddhist holidays vary according to the lunar calendar (➤ 59, Best Festivals). Contact the Tourism Authority of Thailand (TAT) for exact dates or check the *Bangkok Post*, the *Nation* or the *Metro* magazine (➤ 91).

FEBRUARY	*Chinese New Year* (early February): a family occasion; temples are busy, shops close *Maga Puja*: candle-lit processions at *wats*
MARCH	*Kite fights and festivals*: during March and April kite enthusiasts gather at Sanam Luang
APRIL	*Chakri Day* (6 April): celebrates the founding in 1782 of the dynasty that still rules Thailand *Songkran* (12–14 April): the Thai New Year; people throw water at each other for a blessing
MAY	*Royal Ploughing Ceremony* (early May): on Sanam Luang; the start of the rice-planting season *Visaka Puja* (mid-May): celebrates the birth, enlightenment and death of the Buddha
JULY	*Asalha Puja*: marks Buddha's first sermon and the start of a three-month Buddhist Rains Retreat
AUGUST	*HM Queen Sirikit's Birthday* (12 August)
SEPTEMBER	*Moon Festival*: the Chinese community honours the moon goddess
OCTOBER	*Ok Pansa*: marks the end of the three-month Rains Retreat. Monks are presented with new robes and other gifts *Royal Barge Ceremony* (not annual): the king travels with a fleet of spectacular barges to Wat Arun to present new robes to the monks
NOVEMBER	*Golden Mount Fair* (1st week of November) *Loy Krathong* (November full moon): small banana-leaf boats with flowers and candles are floated in honour of water spirits *The Bangkok Marathon* (end of November) *Long-boat races* (end of November): on the river
DECEMBER	*Trooping the Colour* (3 December): starts a week of celebrations to honour HM King Bhumibol's birthday, which falls on 5 December

BANGKOK's
top 25 sights

*These sights are shown on the maps on the inside front cover and inside back cover, numbered **1–25** from west to east across the city*

23

1

ROYAL BARGE MUSEUM

Top and above: elaborate detail on the royal barges

HIGHLIGHTS

- *Suphannahongsa*, the largest of the royal barges
- The serpent-headed prow of *Anantanagaraj*
- View along Klong Bangkok Noi

INFORMATION

During December you might get to see the fabulous gilded barges being rowed across the Chao Phraya to honour King Bhumibol's birthday. Otherwise, use your imagination to bring them alive as they sit in this boathouse museum.

Suphannahongsa Just as royalty now drives around in beautiful cars, so Thai kings used splendidly carved boats as their everyday transport in the days when Bangkok was very much the 'Venice of the East'. The grandest of all the royal boats in the museum, the *Suphannahongsa*, was first used in 1911 by King Rama VI. It is 45m long, intricately carved and gilded, and was reserved exclusively for the king, who sat under the gold canopy in the centre. The prow rears up into a mythical swan-like bird known as a *hongsa*. Manned by more than 50 oarsmen, it must have been a wonderful sight as it passed Wat Arun and the riverfront of the Royal Palace. Once in a while – as, for example, at the commemoration of King Bhumibol's 50th anniversary on the throne in December 1996 – the *Suphannahongsa* and her sister boats are launched on the river as the centrepiece of grand celebrations.

Boats for lesser mortals The second-largest barge in the shed is the *Anantanagaraj*, beautifully carved and with a seven-headed *naga* serpent at its prow. Around it are others from the royal fleet – when 19th-century Thai kings went out, they were accompanied by hundreds of barges. Amongst them is a barge similar to the one sent to greet British diplomat Sir John Bowring, who went to make a trade pact with the king in 1855, which had 'the gilded and emblazoned image of an idol at its prow, with two flags like vanes grandly ornamented...'.

KLONG BANGKOK YAI

One of the best ways to escape the hell of Bangkok's traffic is to take to the water – a swimming pool, a ride on the riverbus or a trip on the canals. Klong Bangkok Yai leads from the Chao Phraya to a host of hidden treasures.

From the river The easiest and cheapest way of getting along Klong Bangkok Yai is on one of the regular long-tail boats from either Tian or Rajini piers on the Chao Phraya. On the right (north) bank as you enter the canal lies Wat Sang Krachai, dating from the Ayutthaya period and restored by early Chakri kings. As you pass under the first of Thonburi's main bridges, look for Wat Welurachin on the left bank, noted for its 19th-century murals. Beyond the next bridge is Wat Inthararam (left bank), containing the ashes of King Taksin, who moved the Siamese capital to Thonburi in 1768 where he was deposed and killed 14 years later. Note the beautiful lacquer decorations on the doors in the ordination hall.

Back to the river At the junction of Klong Sanam Chai and Bangkok Noi sits Wat Pak Nam, a huge temple from the Ayutthaya period, noted for its meditation centre. From here Klong Bangkok Yai curves north until it meets Klong Bang Noi (left) and Klong Mon (right), which leads back to the Chao Phraya river. Continuing straight across this junction, Klong Bangkok Yai is called Klong Chak Phra and leads, in a great arc, to Klong Bangkok Noi, and thence to the Royal Barge Museum and the Chao Phraya river.

HIGHLIGHTS

- Life and boats along the *klongs*
- Murals in Wat Welurachin
- Wat Inthararam's painted doors
- Amulets from Wat Pak Nam

INFORMATION

- ⊞ B9
- 🍴 Floating foodstalls along the *klong* (£)
- 🚤 Boats from Tian and Rajini piers
- ♿ None
- ↔ Royal Barge Museum
  (► 24), Wat Arun
  (► 27), Chao Phraya river
  (► 28)

Top and below: daily pursuits on the river

WAT RA KANG

HIGHLIGHTS

- Woodcarvings in the library
- Murals of the *Ramakien*
- Quiet garden
- Views of the Grand Palace

INFORMATION

- B8
- Soi Wat Ra Kang Khositaram, off Thanon Arun Amarin
- Daily 5AM–9PM
- Express boat to Chang Wang Luang pier, then cross-river ferry to Wat Ra Kang
- None
- Free
- Royal Barge Museum (➤ 24), Wat Arun (➤ 27), Chao Phraya river (➤ 28)

Exceptionally fine murals

Claims that the Ayutthaya period was one of the high points of Thai art are supported by this undervisited temple, peacefully situated on the banks of the river. Its murals and woodcarvings are quite exquisite.

Bell temple Most tourists overlook this delightful smaller *wat*, which dates from the Ayutthaya period, as does its neighbour Wat Arun (➤ 27). King Taksin undertook serious restorations when he settled in Thonburi, and Rama I rebuilt it extensively. *Rakang* means bell, and at 8AM and 6PM every day the *wat's* many bells are rung. The lovely garden feels far removed from bustling Bangkok and is a great place to rest, to enjoy the cross-river view of the Grand Palace or even to meditate.

A royal present The beautiful library in the compound of Wat Ra Kang was a gift from Rama I to the temple after he founded the Chakri Dynasty. He lived in this elegant 18th-century teak building before he became king, and carried out extensive renovations at the time. The building was suffering from neglect a few years ago, and was restored by the Association of Siamese Architects. The stucco and carved wooden doors and window panels are incredibly fine examples of the Ayutthaya style, depicting figures from the epic *Ramakien*, the Thai interpretation of the Indian Hindu *Ramayana* story. Both the doors and the murals on the interior walls – the work of the great priest-painter Phra Acharn Nak – are considered by art historians to be among the finest in Bangkok.

WAT ARUN (TEMPLE OF DAWN)

Despite the competition from numerous skyscrapers fighting for space on Bangkok's horizon, the glittering towers of the Temple of Dawn still rise tall above the river, and the sweeping views from its higher terraces are not to be missed.

The temple of Arun King Taksin chose this 17th-century *wat* for his royal temple and palace as it was the first place in Thonburi to catch the morning light. The Emerald Buddha was housed here after it was recaptured from Laos, before being moved to Wat Phra Keo in 1785. Even without the sacred statue, Wat Arun continued to be much revered, and the kings Rama II and Rama III reconstructed and enlarged it to its present height of 104m. Today, the *wat* has a long, elongated, Khmer-style *prang* (tower), and four minor towers, symbolising Mount Meru, the terrestrial representation of the 33 heavens. The *prangs* are covered with pieces of porcelain, which Chinese boats coming to Bangkok used as ballast.

The main *prang* Steep steps lead to the two terraces that form the base of the *prang* (closed for restoration). The different layers, or heavens, are supported by *kinnari*, or half-humans, and frightening *yakshas*, or demons. Pavilions on the first platform contain statues of the Buddha at the most important stages of his life, while on the second terrace four statues of the Hindu god Indra stand guard.

Exploring Most tourists come for the climb and don't have time for the rest of the *wat*, so it is a quiet place for a stroll. The main Buddha image inside the *bot* (chapel) is believed to have been designed by Rama II himself, but the murals date from the reign of Rama V.

HIGHLIGHTS

- Central *prang*
- Close-up of the Chinese porcelain decorations on the *prangs*
- Main Buddha image inside the *bot*

Statue at the temple, a classic image of the city

INFORMATION

- ✚ B9
- ✉ Thanon Arun Amarin
- 🕐 Daily 8–5:30
- 🍴 Foodstalls on the riverbank
- 🚢 Express boat to Thian pier, then cross-river ferry
- ♿ None
- 💰 Cheap
- ↔ Royal Barge Museum (► 24), Klong Bangkok Yai (► 25), Wat Ra Kang (► 26), Chao Phraya river (► 28), Grand Palace (► 29), Wat Phra Keo (► 30), Wat Po (► 33), Wat Prayoon (► 34)

MAE NAM CHAO PHRAYA

The Chao Phraya river, Bangkok's main artery, is a wonderful balm. To board a boat, sniff the breeze and see the grand buildings lining the banks, is one of the most exciting, unique and soothing experiences in Bangkok.

The river of kings You can learn much about the history of Bangkok from the Chao Phraya, for it is a city that was designed to be seen from the water: a hundred years ago you would have arrived upriver from the sea port rather than across the city from the airport. Besides the Grand Palace, look out for other buildings connected to the present Chakri Dynasty. These include the Royal Barge Museum, remains of two forts, Chakrabongse House, Wat Ra Kang, Sipakorn University, and a couple of royal residences between Krung Thon and Phra Pokklao bridges, one of which was the childhood home of Queen Sirikit.

The river of the people The more congested road traffic becomes, the more people in Bangkok dream of returning to their river. Older inhabitants, in the shadow of the many new glass and concrete highrises, are still living waterborne lives in stilt-houses and on barges, dependent on the brown river for their washing, fishing and transport. People living on barges near Krung Thep Bridge (past the Marriott Royal Garden Riverside Hotel) trade in charcoal, while others work at the rice warehouses across the river. Further upstream, watch out for market traders around Pak Klong Talaat and teak loggers with their goods moored around Krung Thon Bridge, waiting for it to be milled and exported. This is some of the best spectator sport Bangkok has to offer and, happily, you are never far from a choice of refreshment.

GRAND PALACE

The palace, home to the Thai royal family until 1946, is undoubtedly grand, but at times it can be difficult to appreciate its full splendour as so many jewels are cramped into a relatively small area. Still, the overall effect is truly overwhelming.

Dusit Maha Prasad When King Rama I moved from Thonburi to Rattanakosin his plan was to construct an exact copy of the destroyed Ayutthaya. First he built himself a palace and a royal temple, Wat Phra Keo (➤ 30). The oldest buildings are the Maha Montien and the Dusit Maha Prasad, the first brick building (1789) constructed in typical Thai style. Intended as an audience hall, it is now the resting place for deceased royals before the official cremation on Sanam Luang (➤ 32).

Chakri Maha Prasad The magnificent Chakri Maha Prasad, designed by British architects, is often referred to as 'the *farang* (foreigner) with the *chada* (head-dress worn by Thai dancers)', as the main building, in imperial Victorian style, is topped with three Thai spires. The ground floor houses a display of weapons, while on the first floor there is the Throne Hall and impressive Reception Hall. The second floor contains the ashes of members of the royal family.

Other delights The Wat Phra Keo Museum houses tiny Buddha images in precious materials and models showing alterations that have been made to the palace and Wat Phra Keo from their beginnings to the modern day. The Amarin Vinichai Prasad (Coronation Hall), built by Rama I and expanded by Rama II and III, is part of the Maha Montien, and is traditionally the room in which each king spends the night after his coronation.

HIGHLIGHTS

- Chakri Maha Prasad
- The garden
- Wat Phra Keo Museum
- Amarin Vinichai Prasad (Coronation Hall)
- Dusit Maha Prasad

Decoration fit for a king

INFORMATION

- ✛ B8/9
- ✉ Thanon Nophralan
- ☎ 222 8181 ext 40
- ◷ Daily 8:30–12, 1–3:30
- 🍴 Thai restaurant and cafeteria within compound
- 🚌 A/C bus 3, 8, 12, 44
- 🚢 Chang Wang Luang pier
- ♿ Few
- 🎫 Moderate; ticket includes a visit to the Grand Palace, Wat Phra Keo (➤ 30), the Coin Pavilion and Vimanmek Palace (➤ 37)
- ↔ Wat Phra Keo (➤ 30), Sanam Luang (➤ 32), Wat Po (➤ 33), Wat Mahathat (➤ 51)

WAT PHRA KEO

HIGHLIGHTS

● Murals in the Chapel Royal
● The Emerald Buddha
● The upper terrace
● Mural of the *Ramakien*

INFORMATION

✚ B8
✉ Thanon Nophralan
☎ 222 8181 ext 40
🕐 Daily 8:30–12
🚌 A/C bus 3, 8, 12, 44
⛴ Chang Wang Luang pier
♿ None
🎫 Included in entrance to Grand Palace
↔ Chao Phraya river (➤ 28), Grand Palace (➤ 29)

Splendid uniformed demons stand guard

A visit to Wat Phra Keo, the Temple of the Emerald Buddha, reveals some of the most stunning architecture in Southeast Asia. It also explains the very long tradition of firm belief the Thai people have in the Buddhist religion and in their nation.

The Emerald Buddha Wat Phra Keo is the holiest of all Thai *wats*, and the small green-jade statue of the Buddha, high on its golden altar in the Chapel Royal, is the most sacred image in Thailand. When the statue was first found in 1434 it was covered in stucco. Years later, the stucco started to crumble away and several miracles occurred, giving the Buddha a reputation for bringing good fortune. Today, thousands of worshippers pay their respects in front of the statue. The late Ayutthaya-style murals on the surrounding walls depict the lives of Buddha, and the superb door panels with mother-of-pearl inlay illustrate scenes from the *Ramakien*, the Thai version of the Indian *Ramayana*. The golden outer walls and gilded angels reflect the sun, while bells along the roofline give voice to the wind.

More temples and murals On the upper terrace next to the Chapel Royal are three other very sacred buildings: the Royal Pantheon, surrounded by gilded *kinaree* (male) and *kinara* (female) half-human figures; the Library, which holds the *Tripitaka*, the sacred Buddhist scriptures; and the impressive golden Phra Si Ratana *chedi* (pagoda) which houses ashes of Buddha. The nearby model of Angkor Wat is a reminder that Cambodia was once under Thai rule (➤ 10). The whole ground is enclosed by galleries decorated with murals depicting the *Ramakien*.

PIPITAPHAN (NATIONAL MUSEUM)

You'll need at least three hours, but preferably a whole day, to come to terms with this treasure trove of Thai art and archaeology. Most of the buildings in which these superb collections are housed are works of art in their own right.

Main collection The museum, founded in 1874 by King Rama V, is housed in the Palace of Prince Wang Na, originally home to the Second King and part of the Grand Palace (▶ 29). The visit starts with a useful introduction to Thai history. Note the black-stone inscription from Sukhothai, the oldest-known record of the Thai alphabet. Two large modern buildings house the main collection of pre-Thai and Thai sculpture, as well as pieces from elsewhere in Asia. An important exhibit in the southern wing is one of the earliest images of Buddha, from Gandhara in India, and is clearly influenced by classical Greek sculpture. A garage in a nearby building houses the collection of magnificent royal funeral chariots, the most amazing being the *Vejayant Rajarot*, built by Rama I in 1785 and still occasionally used, even though it needs 300 men to pull it.

Palace of Wang Na Built in the 1780s as a home for the king's successor, the palace houses a magnificent collection of Thai art objects. Note in Room 23 a wonderful collection of traditional musical instruments from Southeast Asia.

Buddhaisawan Chapel The Phra Sihing Buddha in this chapel is said to have been divinely created in Sri Lanka and sent to Sukhothai in the 13th century. Despite doubts about its origins (it actually dates from the 15th century), it is still worshipped by many and is carried in procession at the Thai New Year. The fine murals around it (▶ 57) tell the stories of Buddha's lives.

HIGHLIGHTS

- Sukhothai sculpture
- *Vejayant Rajarot* chariot
- Red House
- Phra Sihing Buddha
- Murals in the Buddhaisawan Chapel
- Musical instruments and audio tapes in the Palace of Wang Na
- Bronze Bodhisattva Avalokitesvara from Chaya (room 9)

INFORMATION

- ✚ B7/8
- ✉ Thanon Naphratad
- ☎ 224 1333
- 🕐 Wed–Sun 9–4, but check beforehand as schedule changes
- 🍴 Cafeteria with cheap food
- 🚌 A/C bus 3, 6, 7, 9, 11, 12, 17
- 🚢 Maha Rat pier
- ♿ Few
- 🎫 Cheap
- ↔ Chao Phraya river (▶ 28), Grand Palace (▶ 29), Wat Phra Keo (▶ 30), Sanam Luang (▶ 32), National Theatre (▶ 81)
- ❓ Free English tours start at ticket pavilion on Wed at 9:30AM (Buddhism) and Thu 9:30AM (Thai art and culture); on other days tours are in German, French and Japanese. For information ☎ 224 1333

SANAM LUANG (ROYAL FIELD)

DID YOU KNOW?

- Every Thai city has a foundation stone representing the city spirit (*phii muang*)
- Many buildings have a spirit house, a small version of a traditional Thai house, where the guardian spirit resides
- An unusual shrine near the Hilton in Nai Lert Park contains a spirit house and several huge wooden phalluses

INFORMATION

- ✚ B/C8
- ✉ Thanon Ratchadamnoen Nai
- 🕐 Daily morning–evening. Lak Muang: Mon–Fri 8:30–4:30
- 🍴 Foodstalls, food market
- 🚌 A/C bus 3, 6, 7, 9, 12, 39, 44
- ⛴ Maha Rat or Chang Wang Luang piers
- ♿ Few
- 💲 Free. Lak Muang: cheap
- ↔ Chao Phraya river (➤ 28), Grand Palace (➤ 29), Wat Phra Keo (➤ 30), National Museum (➤ 31)
- ❓ Often Thai traditional dance at Lak Muang around noon. A new trishaw service has been announced to help visitors explore the area

Just north of the Grand Palace are the royal cremation grounds, today most often used for recreation. The Lak Muang, foodstalls and many shady trees can be found here, and it's a great place to relax after an exhausting visit to the adjoining sights.

Royal cremation grounds This vast green field near the Grand Palace was originally designed as the funeral grounds for royal members of the Chakri Dynasty. The last ceremonial cremations, attended by more than 4,000 people, took place in March 1996 for the funeral of the mother of the present King Bhumibol. Sanam Luang is also the site of the annual Ploughing Ceremony, when the king marks the beginning of the rice-growing season, and for the celebrations of King Bhumibol's birthday on 5 December (➤ 22). The statue of the earth goddess, Mae Thorani, in a pavilion on the northern side, was erected by King Chulalongkorn as part of a public fountain.

Lak Muang (City Pillar Shrine) This lovely shrine, believed to be inhabited by the spirit that protects Bangkok, is built around two Sivaite *lingam* wooden pillars erected by Rama I in 1782 to mark the founding of his new capital. Rama V added other idols to the shrine, and today worshippers can be seen here day and night, making offerings of flowers, incense and prepared food. Thai dancers are often commissioned to show gratitude to the guardian deity for granting a wish.

Kite fights The green space is now mainly used for recreation. People come here for family picnics, to rest, to play ball games and to fly kites. There are regular kite competitions between February and May.

WAT PO

After a visit to the Grand Palace or a day's shopping in Chinatown or Siam Square, there's nothing more relaxing than a visit to the beautiful temple compound of Wat Po and a vigorous Thai massage to get you back on your feet.

The Reclining Buddha Wat Po was built in the 16th century during the Ayutthaya period and then almost completely rebuilt in 1781 by Rama I. It is Bangkok's oldest and Thailand's largest *wat*. Thanon Chethuphon divides the grounds in two, one side comprising the temple buildings and the other the monks' quarters. The temple's main attraction is the giant Reclining Buddha, 46m long and 15m high, which represents the dying Buddha lying in the position he adopted to attain nirvana. The statue was built in the 19th century during the reign of Rama III, from brick covered with lacquer, plaster and gold leaf. The soles of the feet are decorated in mother-of-pearl with 108 signs of Buddha. The beautiful *bot*, or central shrine, has delicately carved sandstone panels representing the *Ramakien* and the finest mother-of-pearl inlaid doors. Although Wat Po contains 91 *chedis*, the four most important are dedicated to the first Chakri kings. Visitors can acquire merit by putting a coin in each of the 108 bronze bowls.

Centre of learning Rama III wanted this temple to be used for education, and Thais still consider it their first public university. The murals in the *viharn* and other buildings explain a wide variety of subjects, such as geography, yoga, astrology, science, literature and arts, as well as religion. Today, the temple complex still includes the Traditional Medical Practitioners' Association (➤ 56), which teaches the traditional art of Thai massage and herbal remedies.

The Reclining Buddha (top) and gilded detail (above) at Wat Po

DID YOU KNOW?

- 95 per cent of Thais practise Theravada Buddhism, also known as 'the lesser vehicle'
- The ultimate destination of Theravada Buddhism is nirvana
- Most Thais pray, donate and gain merit at temples in the hope of acquiring rebirth in a better life

INFORMATION

- ✚ B/C9
- ✉ Thanon Maha Rat
- ☎ 225 4771
- ⏰ Daily 8–5, massage until 6
- 🚍 A/C bus 1, 6, 7, 8, 12
- ⛴ Tian pier
- ♿ None
- 💲 Cheap
- ↔ Chao Phraya river (➤ 28), Grand Palace (➤ 29), Wat Phra Keo (➤ 30), Phak Klong Market (➤ 52–3)

WAT PRAYOON

DID YOU KNOW?

- Just upstream of Memorial Bridge is the Catholic Church of Santa Cruz, the core of the old Portuguese quarter
- Several Portuguese churches still exist today, including the Church of the Immaculate Conception (1837) near Krung Thon Bridge and the Holy Rosary Church (1787) near the River City Shopping Complex (➤ 38)

INFORMATION

- ⊞ C10
- ✉ Soi 1, off Thanon Thetsaban
- 🕐 Daily 9–6
- 🚌 A/C bus 6
- ⛴ Saphan Phot pier, then walk over Memorial Bridge
- ♿ None
- 🍴 Free; cheap turtle food
- ↔ Wat Arun (➤ 27), Chao Phraya river (➤ 28)

There is something surreal about this temple complex, lying in the shadow of the old Memorial Bridge, with its giant chedi, *artificial hill of miniature shrines, and turtles partial to the taste of tourist fingers (you have been warned...).*

Wat Prayun Rawongsawat Wat Prayoon, known locally under its longer name of Wat Prayun Rawongsawat, was built during the reign of Rama III by the powerful local Bunnag family. Its huge grey *chedis* (pagodas) are easily recognised from the river and Memorial Bridge. The *wat* has some fine mother-of-pearl inlaid doors.

Turtle Mount To the right as you enter is a man-made hill, circled clockwise by worshippers. It was constructed by King Rama III after he observed the shapes made by candle wax as it melted. Between the strange shapes are shrines to the dead in different styles, from the most traditional Thai-style *chedi* to a cowboy ranch complete with cacti. The thousands of turtles in the pond surrounding the shrines gave the mount its name. Vendors sell bread and fruit for these greedy creatures – locals believe special merit is gained by feeding them. Sticks are available to ensure that the turtles don't eat your fingers too. At the edge of the pond is a memorial to the unfortunate men who died in 1836 when one of the temple's canon exploded.

Siamese twins Bangkok's first European-style house, home of British trader Robert Hunter, used to stand in front of the *wat*. In 1824 Hunter saw the original Siamese twins, Chang and Eng, swimming in the river near here. The twins left Siam in 1829, eventually marrying two American sisters with whom they had 22 children. They died in 1874 within two hours of each other.

WAT SAKET

It's easy to get lost in the grounds of this vast yet peaceful temple, but the short, steep climb up the Golden Mount puts everything back in perspective and offers views over Rattanakosin that are simply stunning.

Golden Mount The main attraction of this temple is the Golden Mount (Phu Khao Thong). The artificial hill, nearly 80m high, was created in the early 19th century after a large *chedi* built by Rama III collapsed when the underlying ground gave way. Only a huge pile of dust and rubble was left, but as Buddhists believe that a religious building should never be destroyed, King Rama IV had 1,000 teak logs put into the foundations. Later, he built a small *chedi* on top of the hill, which is believed to contain Buddha's teeth. During World War II, concrete walls were added to prevent any further erosion. Views from the terrace on top of the hill are wonderful, and visitors are allowed into the golden *chedi*. Every year (first week of November) a fabulous temple fair takes place, when believers hold a solemn candle-lit procession up the illuminated Golden Mount.

Temple complex The temple was built outside the city walls by King Rama I during the late 18th century as the city's main crematorium. The king performed the Royal Hair Bathing Ceremony here before he was crowned. When plague raged through the city in the 19th century, the temple became a charnel house and more than 60,000 victims were left here to the vultures. The temple is still in the process of restoration, but the fine murals that can be seen in the main temple are worth a close inspection. There are two important old Buddha statues in the Shrine Hall.

The chedi, *built on the Golden Mount in 1863*

HIGHLIGHTS

- Views over Rattanakosin
- Murals in the main chapel
- Old Buddha statues
- Temple fair in November
- Tiny bird and antique market

INFORMATION

- ✚ D8
- ✉ Off Thanon Bamrung Muang
- ☎ 223 4561
- 🕐 Daily 7:30 – 5:30
- 🚌 A/C bus 8
- ⛴ Water-taxis along Klong San Sap and Klong Maha Nak
- ♿ None
- 💵 Free; cheap entrance fee for the top of Golden Mount
- ➡ Wat Ratchabopit (➤ 51), Wat Suthat and the Giant Swing (➤ 51)

35

CHINATOWN

HIGHLIGHTS

- Soi Wanit 1 (Sampeng Lane)
- Thanon Yaowarat, or 'Gold Street'
- Chalermkrung Royal Theatre
- Wat Chakrawat
- Nakorn Kasem (Thieves' Market)
- Soi Isaraphap
- Leng Noi Yee Temple

INFORMATION

- D9/10
- Street stalls, food markets, Siang Ping Loh (► 66)
- A/C bus 1, 7
- Ratchawong pier
- Few
- Wat Traimit (► 40)

Chinatown's busy and intricate network of alleyways may no longer be lined with brothels and opium dens, but its amazing markets and temples, the latter shrouded in clouds of incense, still give it the feel of a world apart, even in Bangkok.

The Chinese community By the 14th century Chinese merchants had set up important trading centres in Thailand and were the only foreigners allowed to live within the walls of Ayutthaya. The Chinese were already well established in Bangkok when King Rama I built his capital on their grounds in 1782 and moved them to the Sampeng area. For a long time Chinatown was the city's commercial centre, also gaining notoriety for its brothels, tea-houses and opium dens. Of the theatres in the area, the recently restored Chalermkrung Royal Theatre (► 81) is a perfect example. Chinese temples seem more down to earth than their Thai counterparts, one of the liveliest being Leng Noi Yee (► 17), which means 'Dragon Lotus Temple'. It has Buddhist, Taoist and Confucianist altars, and you will find old Chinese men playing chess and watching the crocodiles in Wat Chakrawat.

Street markets Chinatown reveals its true soul in its street markets, old shophouses and shopping streets. The busiest alleyways are Soi Wanit 1 (Sampeng Lane) and Soi Isaraphap (► 17), and through the heart of it all cuts Thanon Yaowarat, famous for its gold shops. Nakorn Kasem, the so-called Thieves' Market (► 53), may no longer offer bargains but it is still great for a stroll.

PHRA THI NANG WIMANMEK

A tour through Vimanmek Palace, the largest golden teak mansion in the world, gives some insight into the interests of the Thai royal family. The beautiful landscaped gardens are also a great place for whiling away the afternoon heat.

'The Palace in the Clouds' The three-storey mansion was originally built in 1868 as a summer house on the island of Ko Si Chang. It was moved to Dusit in 1901 and, quite understandably, soon became King Rama V's favourite palace, being used as the royal residence between 1902 and 1906. It was closed down in 1935 and remained in this state until Queen Sirikit re-opened it in 1982 as a museum to mark Bangkok's bicentennial celebrations.

Although European influence is clearly visible in the style, Vimanmek is built according to Thai traditions, using golden teak wood and not a single nail. Teak wood contains a special oil which makes it resistant to heat and heavy rains, and which also acts as an insect repellent. Amongst the possessions of Rama V on display is Thailand's first indoor bathroom and the oldest typewriter with Thai characters, as well as Thai ceramics, European furniture, precious china and lovely portraits.

The other pavilions The Royal Carriage Museum contains carriages, mostly imported from Europe, which were very popular at the time of Rama V. The small Suan Farang Kunsai Mansion has oil paintings and pictures of Rama V and his family. The Abhisek Dusit Throne Hall, again built in a harmonious Euro-Thai style, has a display of handicrafts, including *mutmee* silk, nielloware and basketry, made by Queen Sirikit's SUPPORT Foundation.

HIGHLIGHTS

- Guided tour through the house
- Garden and pond
- Trophy Room
- Ivory objects in the library

INFORMATION

- ✚ E6
- ✉ 193/2 Thanon Ratchawithi
- ☎ 281 4715
- 🕐 Daily 9–4 (tickets sold until 3). Visitors wearing shorts or sleeveless shirts may not be admitted as this is a royal property.
  Abhisek Dusit Throne Hall: daily 1–4
- 🍴 Cafeteria in grounds and Thai restaurant near crafts shop
- 🚌 A/C bus 10
- ♿ None
- 💰 Moderate; free with entrance ticket for Grand Palace and Wat Phra Keo (➤ 29 and 30)
- ↔ Dusit Zoo (➤ 60), Chit Lada Palace (home of the royal family; closed to the public)
- ❓ Tours of the palace in English and other languages every half-hour. Free performances of Thai dancing, Thai boxing, and sword- and club-fighting at 10:30AM and 2PM

RIVER CITY SHOPPING COMPLEX

SHOPPING CENTRES

- Fashionable shopping centres (➤ 74, panel)
- Old Siam Plaza (➤ 54)
- Central Department Stores, on Thanon Silom and Thanon Ploenchit, are excellent for underwear, T-shirts, household goods and miscellanea
- Robinson's Department Store, on the corner of Thanon Rama IV and Thanon Silom, sells everything, including food
- Emporium (➤ 74) is the newest and currently the most chic shopping centre

INFORMATION

- ✚ E11
- ✉ 23 Thanon Yotha, off Thanon Sri Phraya
- ☎ 237 0077
- ◷ Daily 10–10. Most shops close around 7 or 8PM, and some close on Sun
- 🍴 Several restaurants, including a coffee-shop, the Savoey Seafood (➤ 65) and a great terrace café
- 🚌 Non-A/C bus 36, 93
- ⛴ Sri Phraya pier
- ♿ Good
- 🎟 Free
- ↔ Chao Phraya river (➤ 28), Chinatown (➤ 36), Oriental Hotel (➤ 39)

Nowadays there are more shopping centres in Bangkok than one can count, but the River City Shopping Complex was the first of its kind on the river and still holds its own as one of the places to look for antiques.

A different experience The River City, adjacent to the Royal Orchid Sheraton, was the first modern air-conditioned shopping centre built on the river. The river again seems to make all the difference, shopping definitely being a less hectic experience here than elsewhere in Bangkok. If you crave the latest Western fashion names or the trendiest bars then River City will look dull and old-fashioned, but if you are looking for fine Thai handicrafts, silks or antiques, there are few better places to go. River City is on the fringes of Chinatown, and on the modern square in front of it the atmosphere is always lively, with foodstalls selling *satay*, fresh fruits and sweet desserts. Local Chinese, hoping for equal good fortune, make offerings at the heavily loaded shrine.

Antiques Thanon Charoen Krung (New Road) and the alleyways around the Oriental Hotel used to be lined with antique shops, but in recent years many of them have moved to the third and fourth floors of River City, which are entirely devoted to the best antiques in town. There is a price to pay for such choice and variety, however: these are some of the most expensive dealers in town. If you do see something you'd like to buy, remember that even though many objects here are priced, it is still customary to haggle. The Auction House on the fourth floor holds an auction every first Saturday of the month; viewings take place on the two preceding Saturdays.

ORIENTAL HOTEL

There are hotels, and then there's the Oriental. Arrive by car, acknowledge the greetings of the hotel's efficient white-uniformed staff, pass through the great glass doors into the lobby and you'll be touched by its magic.

Romantic past Nothing remains of the original 1876 Oriental, but the Authors' Residence, dwarfed by two more modern wings, is the surviving building of 1887. This section contains the hotel's most luxurious suites, named after such illustrious guests as Somerset Maugham, Graham Greene and Noel Coward, and continues to attract modern celebrities such as David Bowie and Tom Cruise. The ground-floor lounge of this colonial building, surrounded by exclusive boutiques, is a great place to escape to on a hot afternoon to take tea.

Luxurious present Elsewhere in the hotel, excellence vies with elegance. If you want to have a look around, go at sunset for a drink on the terrace or an alfresco dinner at the excellent riverside buffet. Alternatively, take the hotel's ferry across the busy river to the Sala Rim Naam for excellent Thai food (➤ 64) and a performace of classical Thai music and dance. If you want to get more involved, there is a world-class cookery school and a cultural programme run by university professors. The luxurious spa, set in a traditional teak house, offers every imaginable treat to soothe or stimulate the body, from the excellent jetlag massage to the papaya body polish and oriental bodywrap, the latter using lemongrass and other medicinal Thai herbs.

DID YOU KNOW?

- The Royal Suite occupies the entire top floor
- It has consistently been voted the world's best hotel

INFORMATION

- E11
- 48 Soi Oriental
- 236 0400
- Excellent restaurants and bar (£££)
- Non-A/C bus 1, 35, 75
- Oriental pier
- Very good
- Wat Arun (➤ 27), Chao Phraya river (➤ 28), River City Shopping Complex (➤ 38)
- Smart casual or business dress. You don't need to stay at the hotel to attend the classes or the spa

Top and below: refined luxury at the Oriental

WAT TRAIMIT

You know when you have arrived at Wat Traimit, the Temple of the Golden Buddha, as the entrance is always blocked with tour buses. But no matter how many tourists invade the space, the Golden Buddha remains as unruffled as ever.

The Golden Buddha The shiny, 3m-tall gold Buddha, which weighs 5.5 tonnes, is believed to be the largest golden Buddha image in the world. The sculpture, made in Sukhothai in the 13th century, was covered with stucco to protect it from the Burmese invaders of the 18th century. It wasn't until 1955, when workmen moved the Buddha image to a new building and saw through some cracks that there was something shining beneath the surface, that the stucco was taken off and solid gold revealed. The discovery sparked a national treasure hunt, but nothing of similar value was found. Historically, the Golden Buddha has nothing to do with the Chinese community, but it seems more than appropriate that it has found its home in Chinatown, which is, after all, the centre of Bangkok's gold trade. The statue is now valued at US$14 million, and several bits of stucco are on display to the left of it.

Top: the Golden Buddha
Right: a less valuable gold-leaf version

A less impressive temple The temple itself probably dates from the early 13th century. The statue of the late abbot, Rev Phra Visutha-Thibordee, who ordered the construction of the new temple for the Golden Buddha, sits just opposite it and is covered in gold leaf.

BAAN JIM THOMPSON

Although it is a great introduction to traditional Thai architecture, Jim Thompson's House clearly shows Western influences. The landscaped garden and views over the **klong** *offer a welcome surprise after bustling Siam Square.*

The lost adventurer American architect Jim Thompson first came to Thailand during World War II. As he couldn't get used to his uneventful life back in New York after the war, he decided to make Thailand his home. Thai culture and crafts fascinated him, but the day he discovered some silk-weavers near his house (▶ 72, panel) his fortune was secured. He was already something of a legend when, in 1967, he disappeared mysteriously during an afternoon walk in the Cameroon Highlands in Malaysia, never to be seen again. Thompson's friend, the prolific author William Warren, wrote a great account of his life and death, *Jim Thompson: The Legendary American of Thailand* (Jim Thompson Thai Silk Co, Bangkok 1970).

Thai-style residence Thompson bought six traditional teak houses in northern and central Thailand, and had them reassembled in Bangkok as his residence, adding Western elements such as stairways and marble floors. The exterior walls were turned inside out to face the interior, and the garden was lovingly landscaped, creating the effect of a peaceful but abundant oasis.

A wonderful collection The spirit of the house, kept as Thompson left it, makes an ideal background for his small but gorgeous display of Asian art. The collection of traditional Thai paintings is one of the best in the world and there are also some very rare Buddha images.

One of the many Asian works of art Thompson acquired on his travels

HIGHLIGHTS

- Teak Thai architecture
- Exotic landscaped garden
- Views over the *klong*
- Asian art collection
- Traditional Thai paintings

INFORMATION

- ✚ F8
- ✉ Soi Kasem San 2, off Thanon Rama I
- ☎ 215 0122
- 🕐 Mon–Sat 9–4:30
- 🚌 A/C bus 8
- 🚤 Water-taxi from Wat Saket (▶ 35) along Klong San Sap
- ♿ None
- 💲 Expensive (guided tours only)
- ↔ Wat Pathum Wanaram (▶ 57)

THANON PATPONG

Patpong – three parallel streets running between Thanon Silom and Thanon Surawong – has a reputation as the centre of all sexual evils, but these days it has cleaned up its act a bit and provides entertainment for a wider audience.

The streets that never sleep Patpong is busy day and night. By day it's another Bangkok shopping street of bookshops, pharmacies and supermarkets. Late in the afternoon, foodstalls set up at either end of Patpong, some of them good enough to be reviewed in the city's Thai-language papers. Then tapes and CDs, cotton clothes (some very good value), fake watches and souvenirs are laid out on Soi Patpong 1. Later, as the street fills with foreigners, the go-go bars open their doors.

Sex trade Patpong's go-go and sex bars cater both to Thais and to *farangs* (foreigners). They and their rivals in places such as Soi Cowboy came into their own in the 1960s when US servicemen on leave from Vietnam created a huge demand for sex workers. In the standard go-go bar, girls in tiny bikinis dance around poles above the bar, while others around the tables hope to persuade a client to buy them a drink (they make a commission) and perhaps take them on elsewhere. More explicit sex bars, whose 'menus' include such items as 'girl with razor blades' and 'girl with cigarette', are usually off the main street and charge more. Note that prostitution is illegal in Thailand, and that the government has recently cracked down severely on child prostitution (➤ panel). Several ordinary bars have now opened in Patpong: there are no scantily clad dancers in places such as Peppermint, where Thai girls are usually outnumbered by foreign girls and their partners.

DID YOU KNOW?

- Child prostitution laws were strengthened in 1994; their clients now face a minimum of four years in prison, with a maximum penalty of life imprisonment
- A recent survey by the Thai Red Cross put the number of prostitutes in Thailand at between 120,000 and 200,000; other estimates are as high as 2 million
- Parents now risk prosecution for selling their children into prostitution
- It is estimated that 2 per cent of the reproductive age group in Thailand is infected with Aids, and 14–15 per cent of prostitutes

INFORMATION

- G11
- Soi Patpong 1, 2, 3, 4, between Thanon Silom and Thanon Surawong
- Most atmospheric after sunset until late at night
- Numerous good restaurants (➤ 62–9) and countless foodstalls
- A/C bus 2, 4, 5, 15
- None
- Lumphini Park (➤ 45)

WANG SUAN PAKKARD

The Suan Pakkard Palace is a haven of peace amidst urban sprawl, and it never fails to delight the few visitors who come its way. Like Jim Thompson (➤ 41), its owners were passionate collectors of Thai arts and traditional architecture.

'Cabbage Farm Palace' Prince and Princess Chumbhot of Nakhon Sawan moved these five traditional Thai houses from Chiang Mai (some of them had belonged to the prince's great-grandfather) in 1952. The cabbage garden was turned into one of Bangkok's finest landscaped gardens and is calm in a uniquely Eastern way. The princess was one of the country's most dedicated art collectors, and the house has been turned into a museum displaying everyday objects such as perfume bottles, betel-nut boxes and musical instruments. Antiques include an exquisite Buddha head from Ayutthaya, Khmer statues and European prints of old Siam.

Ban Chiang House An entire house has been devoted to the elegant pottery and bronze jewellery discovered at Ban Chiang, an important Bronze Age settlement in northern Thailand, dating from around 1600–500 BC. The ground floor houses a large collection of minerals and sea shells, mostly from Thailand.

Lacquer Pavilion The exquisite Lacquer Pavilion, once part of an Ayutthaya monastery, was moved here in 1958 as a birthday present from the prince to the princess. The remarkable gold and black lacquer murals, painstakingly restored, depict events from the life of the Buddha and the *Ramakien*, the Thai version of the Indian *Ramayana* epic. The lower layer is notable for its representations of daily life, including the odd *farang* on horseback.

HIGHLIGHTS

- Lacquer Pavilion
- Buddha head from Ayutthaya
- Lovely enclosed garden
- Wonderful prints of old Siam by European artists
- Grumpy old pelican in the garden

INFORMATION

- ✚ G8
- ✉ 352 Thanon Sri Ayudhaya
- ☎ 245 4934
- ⏰ Mon–Sat 9–4
- 🍽 Restaurants around Victory Monument
- 🚌 A/C bus 2, 3, 13
- ♿ None
- 🎫 Moderate

The collection of fine art extends into the grounds

SAAN PHRA PHROM (ERAWAN SHRINE)

DID YOU KNOW?

- Thai Buddhism is syncretic as it incorporates elements of Brahmanism, animism and ancestor worship
- A spirit house's location is determined by a Brahmin priest

INFORMATION

- ✚ H9
- ✉ Corner of Thanon Ratchadamri and Thanon Ploenchit
- 🕐 Early morning–late night
- 🍽 Restaurants in nearby hotels and shopping malls
- 🚌 A/C bus 1, 4, 5, 8, 11, 13, 15
- 🚻 Few
- 💲 Free
- ↔ Lumphini Park (► 45)

The shrine is always strewn with offerings

Surrounded by Bangkok's trendiest stores, the Erawan Shrine comes as something of a surprise. And yet the old ways of praying and making offerings do blend in with the new money culture. Atmospheric classical dancing can be seen here for free.

Spirit house The Erawan Shrine was erected as a spirit house (► 32, panel) connected to the Erawan Hotel, which has now made way for the Grand Hyatt Erawan Hotel. The forces of the typical Thai spirit house didn't seem effective enough during the building of the hotel, so spirit doctors advised that it be replaced with the four-headed image of Brahma (Phra Phrom in Thai). There have been no further hitches since then, and the shrine has became famous for bringing good fortune. The name Erawan comes from Brahma's three-headed elephant.

Merit-making People offer colourful flower garlands, lotus flowers, incense and candles; after a few minutes at the shrine your senses tend to go into overdrive. Often, if a wish has been granted, people thank the spirits by donating teak elephants or commissioning the classical dancers and live orchestra. Outside the shrine women sell birds in tiny cages, which are believed to bring good fortune and earn merit if you set them free. Lottery tickets sold by handicapped vendors at the shrine are thought to be particularly lucky. The variety of worshippers is also surprising: older people set in their ways, middle-class Thai families with children, and fashionable younger women in the latest Western designer clothes all kneel down to perform the same traditional rites.

22

SUAN LUMPHINI (LUMPHINI PARK)

At first sight the park looks rather sad and dusty. But spend time in this demanding city and the value of Lumphini will become apparent. It is one of the places that keep people sane, and also allows valuable insight into how Thais relax.

The park is a peaceful oasis in the hectic city

First light Lumphini is a place of moods rather than sights. In the early morning it's full of people exercising. More striking and graceful than the joggers are Chinese-led *t'ai chi* groups, making slow movements to music. At this hour traders also sell snake blood, a powerful tonic. Suddenly, all this activity comes to an abrupt halt and everyone stands to attention as the PA system plays the national anthem. By 9AM, when the sun is up and rush-hour traffic is souring the air, the crowd thins out.

Last light There's a different crowd in the afternoon. Joggers run on the 2.5km track, people pump weights at the open-air gym and, in the windy season (Feb–Apr), kites soar above the busy city – at the height of the season you can buy beautiful kites here. When the light softens so does the atmosphere. Couples come out, foodstalls are set up and boats are rowed on the man-made lake until, at 6PM, with traffic at a halt in the evening rush, people in the park also come to a standstill as the national anthem is played again. The park is especially atmospheric at dusk, when the skyscrapers are silhouetted against the fading light.

DID YOU KNOW?

● Lumphini is Bangkok's biggest inner city park. Other green spaces in the city include: Chatuchak Park, near the weekend market (➤ 46); Vimanmek Palace garden (➤ 37); Sanam Luang (➤ 32); and the Hilton International at Nai Lert Park (the hotel has preserved much of the gardens of the grand old house it has replaced)

INFORMATION

✚ Main entrance: H10/11
✉ Corner of Thanon Rama IV and Thanon Ratchadamri
🕐 Daily 5AM – 8PM
🍴 Restaurant and foodstalls (£–££)
🚌 A/C bus 2, 4, 5, 7, 15
♿ Very good
💵 Free
🔁 Shopping at World Trade Center and Peninsula Plaza (➤ 74, panel), Erawan Shrine (➤ 44), Thanon Sukhumwit (➤ 47)
❓ The boating concession is open 6AM – 8PM

CHATUCHAK WEEKEND MARKET

HIGHLIGHTS

- Amulets and collectors' items, section 1
- Old photos, section 2
- Hill-tribe textiles and crafts, sections 22–6
- Aw Taw Kaw Market, royal project for organically grown produce on other side of Thanon Phahonyothin

Local crafts galore can be found at this huge market

INFORMATION

- ✚ J3
- ✉ Thanon Phahonyothin, near Chatuchak Park
- 🕐 Sat–Sun 9–6
- 🍴 Foodstalls, D'Jit Pochana (➤ 63), Chamlong Vegetarian Restaurant (£) near bus terminal
- 🚍 A/C bus 2, 3, 10, 13, 29
- ♿ None
- ❓ TAT office ✉ Off Thanon Kampong Phet 2

This weekend market feels like the mother of all markets, and if you know where to look you can find everything from baby crocodiles and children's clothes to mutmee *silk pyjamas and household equipment.*

General view It used to take an hour (or even longer) to get to the market from the city centre, but it is now much faster with the new expressway. Before going, get hold of Nancy Chandler's *Map of Bangkok* (available from English-language bookshops), which has a detailed map of Chatuchak showing what is on sale where. Some stalls are aimed at tourists, but most cater to Thais who come here looking for food, plants, furnishings or clothes, or simply for a drink.

Everything on sale If time is limited, start with Sois 1, 2, 3 and 4, which sell mainly antiques, woodcarvings, musical instruments, hill-tribe items and crafts. The selection of old and new sarongs in cotton and *mutmee* silk is amazing, while clothes by young Thai designers are very wearable. The sections around the clocktower have mainly food supplies and, on the other side, household items and live animals.

Illegal trade Regardless of a Thai law protecting endangered species, some endangered animals are still on sale in Chatuchak, branded 'the wildlife supermarket of the world' by the Worldwide Fund for Nature. Very few endangered animals are now openly on sale in the market and, if they are, their cages will have signs insisting on 'No Photograph'. However, the black market is still thriving, and apparently animals such as crocodiles, gibbons, tigers and lion cubs are still on sale to be eaten for their supposed medicinal properties, or as pets.

THANON SUKHUMWIT

Sukhumwit Road runs like a long artery through the heart of modern Bangkok, but the traffic does not always flow. In the rush hour you can easily get stuck in traffic for an hour or more, in which case the only solution might be to get out and shop.

The wealthy *farang* area At its start it is called Thanon Rama I, beyond Siam Square it becomes Thanon Ploenchit and past the bridge of the expressway it finally becomes Thanon Sukhumwit. Several up-market shopping malls line Thanon Ploenchit and quite a few of the older embassies lie just off it. Where once *farangs* (foreigners) preferred to live near the Chao Phraya river, most now live on the *sois* off Thanon Sukhumwit in pretty villas with gardens or in luxurious apartment blocks.

Shopping The small streets around Sukhumwit Soi 23 have some of the trendiest shops in town, and away from the traffic they make for a pleasant stroll. In particular, look out for Rasi Sayam (► 75); Gifted Hands (► 75); and Thailand's answer to Habitat, Homework (► 75, panel). Also near by are the Siam Society and Baan Kam Thieng (► 48), while back on Sukhumwit is the up-market Emporium Shopping Centre, some excellent cinemas and numerous restaurants.

Art galleries The contemporary art scene has mostly moved away from the Sukhumwit area (► 75), but a few galleries are still worth checking out. The Grand Hyatt Erawan Hotel on Thanon Ratchadamri and the Landmark Hotel on Sukhumwit have important collections exhibited on a rotational basis, while the 2 Oceans 23 Gallery and Carpediem Galleries on Soi Thonglor show work from Thai artists and from foreign artists based in Thailand.

DID YOU KNOW?

- *Thanon* means 'road', *soi* means 'small street' and *drok* means 'little alley'
- Some *soi* are also known under their proper names – for example, Sukhumwit Soi 21 is Soi Asoke

INFORMATION

- J9–K10 and off map
- Numerous good restaurants
- A/C bus 1, 8, 11, 13
- Few
- Jim Thompson's House (► 41), Erawan Shrine (► 44), Baan Kam Thieng (► 48)
- 2 Oceans 23 ✉ 18/3 Sukhumwit Soi 23 ☎ 259 9425 🕙 Daily 10–4. Carpediem Galleries ✉ 806/1–3 Soi Thonglor ☎ 714 9903 🕙 Daily 10–5

Sukhumwit traffic

BAAN KAM THIENG

> *Kam Thieng House, a 19th-century teak stilt-house from Chiang Mai, is becoming increasingly encroached upon by the city. However, its collection gives an interesting glimpse of the rural lifestyle of northern Thailand.*

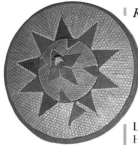

Traditional headwear on show in the museum

HIGHLIGHTS

- Siam Society Library
- Strange floral lintels above the door to the inner room to ward off evil spirits
- An encounter with the spirits of the three elderly women

INFORMATION

- ⊕ K9/10
- ✉ 131 Sukhumwit Soi 21 (Soi Asoke)
- ☎ 661 6470
- 🕐 Tue–Sat 9–12, 1–5. English-language guided tours Sat 9:30AM
- 🍴 Drinks in cafeteria
- 🚌 A/C bus 1, 8, 11, 13
- ♿ None
- 💵 Cheap
- ↔ Thanon Sukhumwit (► 47)
- ❓ The Siam Society has a library, gallery and small office selling its books. For lectures, check the society's programme or local English-language papers

Lanna Living Museum Unlike Jim Thompson's House (► 41) and the Suan Pakkard Palace (► 43), Baan Kam Thieng shows how ordinary people lived. It represents a complete northern Thai house with living quarters, kitchen, well, granary, rice pounder, spirit house, and household objects and utensils used in the daily life of the people of the north. Farming tools and fish traps are displayed on the ground level, while upstairs rooms give a feel of the rural lifestyle of 150 years ago. The house was built by the granddaughter of a wealthy northern prince, and it is believed that her spirit and the spirit of her mother and granddaughter still inhabit the house: there are many stories of inexplicable incidents occurring here.

Saengaroon House The more recently acquired Saengaroon House, originally from Ayutthaya, contains the craft collection of the Thai architect Saengaroon Ratagasikorn, who studied in the USA under Frank Lloyd Wright. He became fascinated with the design of farm implements: simple and beautiful yet still functional.

Siam Society The lovely garden belongs to the Siam Society, which also has an excellent library, highly recommended for anyone interested in Thai culture (call before visiting). The society also supports a gallery, holds lectures, organises cultural trips throughout the country, and publishes interesting books on Thai culture and nature as well as the *Journal of the Siam Society*.

BANGKOK's
best

TEMPLES

Wat Phra Keo

Thai meditation

Some Thai temples provide Vipassana or 'insight' meditation sessions in English. For more information check with:

• World Fellowship of Buddhists (WFB) ✉ 33 Thanon Sukhumwit, between Soi 1 and 3 ☎ 251 1188.

• International Buddhist Meditation Centre (BMC) ✉ Mahachulalongkorn Buddhist University, Wat Mahadhatu, Ta-Prachan ☎ 222 2835 ext 130.

See Top 25 Sights for
WAT ARUN (► 27)
WAT PHRA KEO (► 30)
WAT PO (► 33)
WAT PRAYOON (► 34)
WAT RA KANG (► 26)
WAT SAKET (► 35)
WAT TRAIMIT (► 40)

WAT BENJAMABORPIT

The 'Marble Temple', the most recent of royal *wats*, is built from Carrara marble in a strange blend of traditional Thai temple architecture and European designs. The courtyard houses a collection of Buddha images from all over Asia. It is an excellent place to watch religious festivals and moonlit processions. Unlike most other temples, monks don't go out seeking alms but are instead visited by merit-makers between 6 and 7AM.

✚ E7 ✉ Thanon Sri Ayudhaya and Thanon Rama V ⏰ Daily 8–5 🍴 Foodstalls 🚌 A/C bus 3 💲 Cheap

WAT KANLAYA NIMIT

The decaying main building, dating from the reign of King Rama III, houses a massive seated Buddha image as well as the largest bronze bell in Thailand.

🔳 B9 ✉ Near the entrance to Klong Bangkok Yai ⏰ Daily during daytime 🚌 A/C bus 6 ⛴ Saphan Phot pier, then walk across Memorial Bridge 🎫 Free

WAT MAHATHAT

Wat Mahathat, one of the older shrines in Bangkok with a relic of Buddha, is home to Mahachulalongkorn University, an important Buddhist meditation and study centre. Some programmes are organised for English-speaking visitors (ask at the Section 5 office for more information). On Sundays and Buddhist festivals a fascinating market is held on the precincts.

🔳 B8 ✉ Thanon Naphratad, near the Grand Palace ⏰ Daily 9–5 🍴 Foodstalls in market 🚌 A/C bus 3, 6, 8, 12, 39 ⛴ Maha Rat pier 🎫 Free

WAT RATCHABOPIT

An unusual *wat*, built around 1870 by King Rama V, with very elaborate decoration. The mother-of-pearl doors and windows of the *bot* (chapel) are especially refined, and the hand-painted tiles clearly show European influence.

🔳 C8 ✉ Thanon Ratchabopit, off Thanon Atsadang ⏰ Daily 8 – 8 🚌 A/C bus 1, 7, 8 ⛴ Tian pier 🎫 Free

WAT RATNADA

The strangest structure in this temple compound is Loha Prasad, or the Iron Monastery, a pink structure with weird metal spires. Bangkok's biggest amulet market is held daily on a nearby compound, and the stalls also sell other objects to ward off evil spirits.

🔳 D8 ✉ Off Thanon Maha Chai, opposite Wat Saket ⏰ Daily 9–5 🍴 Foodstalls 🚌 A/C bus 8, 11, 12, 39, 44 🎫 Free

WAT SUTHAT

In Bangkok's tallest *viharn* (religious hall), at Wat Suthat, is housed a 14th-century Buddha statue from Sukhothai surrounded by depictions of the Buddha's last 24 lives. The courtyard is filled with odd statues of scholars and sailors, brought as ballast in rice boats returning from China, while the doors of the *wat* are said to have been carved by King Rama II. In an annual ceremony to celebrate the rice harvest that was still observed just before World War II, men used to ride on the Giant Swing and try to grab a bag of silver coins attached to a pole; only the teak arch remains.

🔳 C8 ✉ Off Thanon Bamrung Muang, opposite the Giant Swing ⏰ Weekends and public holidays only 9–5 🍴 Foodstalls 🚌 A/C bus 8 🎫 Free

Amulets (*phra phim*)

Amulets, often made by monks, depict images of Buddha, revered holy men or famous monks. People choose their amulets very carefully as they are believed to have magical powers, the strength of which depends on the amulet's history or maker. Amulets come in various prices and with specific qualities: some promise a happy love life or fertility, while others will protect against particular illnesses or bring good luck.

Wat Benjamaborpit

51

MARKETS

Shopping map

If you've come to Bangkok to shop till you drop in the markets, or if you're looking for something more specialised – that quaint little store selling hand-made papers, *satay* grills or Chinese calendars – under no circumstances set off without Nancy Chandler's *Map of Bangkok*. The map, available from most English-language bookshops, covers Bangkok's main markets and shopping streets, highlighting the best, as well as the most unusual sights, known only to long-term residents.

Up-country market

If the city gets to you, take the Chao Phraya express boat northwards and get out at the last stop to visit the great market in Nonthaburi, the first town north of Bangkok. The trip itself is fun, passing rice barges, stilt-houses and other common river sights. The market has a provincial feel and is known for its excellent fruits, especially the smelly durian, grown in local orchards (➤ 58, Klong Om).

See Top 25 Sights for
CHATUCHAK WEEKEND MARKET (➤ 46)
KLONG BANGKOK YAI, FLOATING MARKET (➤ 25)
See Walks for
CHINATOWN (➤ 17)
See Evening Strolls for
PATPONG AND SUKHUMVIT NIGHT MARKETS (➤ 18)

BANG RAK MARKET

Although becoming increasingly confined, Bang Rak is still regarded as the best of the city's fruit and vegetable markets, with produce fresh from the gardens and orchards of Thonburi across the river.
🚏 E11 ✉ Thanon Charoen Krung (New Road), near Shangri-La Hotel ⏰ Daily 🍴 Foodstalls 🚌 A/C bus 15 ⛴ Oriental pier

BANGLAMPHOO MARKET

A huge market area with street vendors – selling all manner of travellers' essentials and extremely cheap clothing – as well as more up-market department stores.
🚏 C7 ✉ Around Thanon Chakkaphong, Thanon Phra Sumen and Thanon Tanao, Thanon Khao San area ⏰ Daily morning–evening 🍴 Thanon Ram Buttri has several open-air Thai restaurants 🚌 A/C bus 6 ⛴ Phra Atit pier

PHAHURAT

Phahurat, the centre of Bangkok's Indian community, is one long continuation of cloth merchants, selling everything (bar Thai silk) from saris and wedding fabrics to curtain and furnishing fabrics.
🚏 C9 ✉ Around Thanon Phahurat ⏰ Daily 🍴 Royal India Restaurant (➤ 67) 🚌 A/C bus 1, 7 ⛴ Saphan Phot pier

PHAK KLONG MARKET

This garden of delights is Bangkok's main market for cut flowers, with baskets full of perfumed lotus, jasmine and orchids. Boats dock here laden with fresh

Dried fish for sale in a street market

vegetables and fruits; these are sold immediately to restaurants and greengrocers.

🔲 C9 ✉ Thanon Chak Phet, on Chao Phraya river near Memorial Bridge 🕓 Daily almost 24 hours 🚌 A/C bus 6 ⛴ Saphan Phot pier

PRATHUNAM

A central market covering a large area and excellent if you are looking for cheaper fabrics. There are also plenty of seamstresses and tailors at hand to make up the outfit of your dreams in a few hours. Locals come for cheap jeans and casual wear, as well as fresh produce and other essentials. Bargaining is a must.

🔲 H8 ✉ Thanon Ratchaphrarop, north of Thanon Phetburi 🕓 Daily morning – evening 🍴 Foodstalls 🚌 A/C bus 4, 13, 15

THEWET FLOWER MARKET

Lovely, quiet flower and plant market on a canal lined with beautiful old houses. The thousands of exotic plants on offer here, not to mention the incredible variety of orchids, make it a must for plant lovers. Even better with the book *Gardening in Bangkok* by M R P Amranand, available from the Siam Society (➤ 48).

🔲 D6 ✉ Klong Phadung Krung Kasem, off Thanon Samsen 🕓 Daily 🍴 Foodstalls 🚌 A/C bus 5, 6 ⛴ Thewet pier

THIEVES' MARKET (NAKORN KASEM)

This corner of Chinatown has its own distinct atmosphere. The narrow lanes are full of shops selling old and new 'antiques', as well as brass and musical instruments such as gongs and heavy bronze drums.

🔲 D9 ✉ Between Thanon Yaowarat, Thanon Boripat and Thanon Chakkawat 🕓 Mon–Sat 🍴 Foodstalls 🚌 A/C bus 1, 7, 8

Floating markets are one of the city's most appealing attractions

53

ARCHITECTURE

Until a few years ago, the roofs and *chedis* (pagodas) of temples dominated Bangkok's skyline, but since the building boom of the mid-1980s skyscrapers are a much more obvious feature. Before the collapse of the Thai economy in 1997, locals joked that every day a higher hotel, condominium or office block went up. Since then many construction and finance companies have gone bankrupt and the city is littered with unfinished buildings.

Thai style

In the late 19th and early 20th centuries, Thai architects mixed European style with traditional Thai forms to produce buildings such as the Vimanmek Palace (➤ 37) and Wat Benjamaborpit (➤ 50). Contemporary architects are doing it again today and producing equally exciting and uniquely Thai buildings.

Window from Wat Benjamaborpit, showing European influence

Books

• Hoskin, John and Hopkins, Allen W, *Bangkok by Design: Architectural Diversity in the City of Angels* (Asia Books, Bangkok 1995).

• Warren, William and Tettoni, Luca, *Thai Style* (Asia Books, Bangkok 1988).

BANK OF ASIA

This famous high-tech space-age building was designed by leading architect Sumet Jumsai.
✚ F12 ✉ Thanon Satorn Tai, between the St Louis and Bang Rak hospitals 🕐 Mon–Fri 8:30–3:30 🚌 A/C bus 5

CHALERMKRUNG ROYAL THEATRE

Next door to the Old Siam Plaza is this recently restored theatre. Built in the 1930s, it is one of Bangkok's few examples of Thai deco.
✚ C9 ✉ Corner of Thanon Charoen Krung (New Road) and Thanon Tripetch ☎ 222 0434 🕐 ➤ 81 for performance details 🚌 A/C bus 1, 7, 8 ⛴ Saphan Phot pier

GRAND HYATT ERAWAN HOTEL

The most flamboyant example of the neo-Thai style has produced a pompous and overpowering blend of Thai styles and classical Western architecture.
✚ H9 ✉ 494 Thanon Ratchadamri ☎ 254 1234 🍴 Restaurants 🚌 A/C bus 4, 5, 15

OLD SIAM PLAZA

This shopping mall in the heart of Chinatown reintroduces the old Bangkok school of architecture, where Thai and European styles influenced traditional Chinese shophouse designs.
✚ C9 ✉ Corner of Thanon Phahurat and Thanon Tripetch 🕐 Mon–Sat 9–6 🍴 Restaurants and street stalls 🚌 A/C bus 1, 7 ⛴ Saphan Phot pier

REGENT HOTEL

The modern, grand interior of the Regent incorporates many traditional Thai designs. The vast murals were painted by the late contemporary master Paiboon Suwanakudt.
✚ H9 ✉ 155 Thanon Ratchadamri ☎ 251 6127 🍴 Excellent restaurants 🚌 A/C bus 4, 5, 15

SUKHOTHAI HOTEL

The 1990s Sukhothai re-uses shapes and motifs from Thailand's medieval capital and has surrounded them with gardens, lotus pools and grand-scale symmetry.
✚ H11 ✉ 13/3 Thanon Satorn Tai ☎ 287 0222 🍴 Excellent restaurants (➤ 62 and ➤ 69, panel) 🚌 A/C bus 5

PLACES TO WATCH THE CITY

ERAWAN SHRINE
This is a good place to see how important religion is for most Thais. No matter how Westernised Thais look or behave, religion is still central to their lives, so here you'll see women in Chanel suits praying and offering flowers (➤ 44).

GOLDEN MOUNT
To view the grandeur of the Royal City of Rattanakosin, climb up the golden *chedi* on this 78m-high hill (➤ 35).

LUMPHINI PARK
Come to the park between 5 and 7AM to view a healthier Bangkok, as Chinese practise *t'ai chi*, young Thais sweat at their aerobic classes and joggers pound the track. In the late afternoon, hire a boat and go rowing across the lake and watch the often dramatic skyline (➤ 45).

SANAM LUANG
In season (February–May/June) on lazy but breezy afternoons, head to the Royal Field to watch the kite sellers, the kite fighters and their supporters get carried away with their pastime (➤ 32).

TERRACE, ORIENTAL HOTEL
The most elegant place in Bangkok to enjoy an early evening drink. Watch the sun set over Thonburi and the river (➤ 39).

THANON PATPONG (PATPONG ROAD)
If you come to this area after the sun has gone down, it soon becomes clear that Bangkok never sleeps. Everyone comes here for *sanuk* (fun) in the bars, markets and street stalls. Nearby Thanon Silom also changes character after dark as the daytime business atmosphere makes way for evening entertainment. Foodstalls along the street's south side are packed to capacity with students, office workers and extended families (➤ 18 and 42).

TIARA ROOM, DUSIT THANI HOTEL
The top-floor Tiara Room commands sweeping views over Lumphini Park and the amazing, transforming Bangkok skyline. For the most dramatic panoramas come at night or sunset (➤ 84).

WAT ARUN
Tackle the steep stairs up the central tower for a magnificent view over the Chao Phraya river (➤ 27); closed for restoration at time of writing.

Views from Wat Arun extend across the river

More books
- Baker, Chris and Pasuk Phongpaichit, *Thailand's Boom!* (Silkworm Books, Chiang Mai 1996). Informative and entertaining book written by a Thai economist and a British historian.
- Somtow, S P, *Jasmine Nights* (Penguin Books, London 1995). Novel about a boy growing up on an estate off Sukhumwit and his adventures into the *klongs* (canals).
- Warren, William, *Bangkok's Waterways* (Asia Books, Bangkok 1989). Entertaining tour of the river and *klongs*.
- Waugh, Alec, *Bangkok, Story of a City* (Little Brown, Boston 1971). History of the city.

MASSAGES

Massage as a healing art is an ancient tradition, but these days the term is more loosely applied

Thai massage

Thai curative massage was probably brought from India by Buddhist monks, and for centuries it has been used to help alleviate various illnesses and ailments. The massage consists of controlled application of pressure by the masseur's hands to stimulate blood circulation. It also uses fresh-herb bags rolled onto certain parts of the body. Most massages offered to tourists are of a different nature, with an oiled masseuse rolling over her clients. For several reasons, it is usually worth looking for the real thing.

BUATIP THAI MASSAGE

Modern centre offering more up-market traditional Thai massage, with a few blind masseurs who, according to connoisseurs, are the best because of their increased tactile sensitivity. There is another branch near the River City Shopping Complex (✉ 672/4 Thanon Sri Phraya ☎ 234 8444).
✚ J9 ✉ 4/13 Sukhumwit Soi 5, opposite Landmark Hotel ☎ 255 1045 ⊙ 10AM–midnight 🚍 A/C bus 1, 8, 11, 13 💷 Minimum 350B per hour

THE MARBLE HOUSE

Traditional Thai massage provided in small cubicles, also with a few blind masseurs available.
✚ G11 ✉ Soi Surawong Plaza, opposite Montien Hotel ☎ 235 3519 ⊙ 1PM–midnight 🚍 A/C bus 2 💷 350B, two hours minimum

ORIENTAL HEALTH SPA

Traditional massages and just about every other body-relaxing treat imaginable. The excellent 'jet-lag massage' is particularly recommended (➤ 39).
✚ E11 ✉ Oriental Hotel, Thonburi side 🍴 Thai spa cuisine 🚍 A/C bus 1, 35, 75 ⛴ Oriental pier ♿ Very good 💷 Expensive

THE THERAPEUTIC AND HEALING MASSAGE COURSE

A first course teaches the ethics and rules of massage and basic techniques for relieving fatigue and tension. The second course goes into advanced techniques for pain relief, muscular problems and nervous tension.
✚ B/C9 ✉ Wat Po Traditional Medical School, Wat Po, Thanon Sanam Chai, Tian pier, Bangkok 10200 ☎ 225 4771 ⊙ Each course takes 30 hours over 15 days, to be arranged with teacher 🚍 A/C bus 6, 7, 8, 44 ⛴ Tian pier 💷 4,500B

TRADITIONAL MEDICAL PRACTITIONERS' ASSOCIATION CENTER

The best and the cheapest place to experience a traditional massage is at this centre on the Wat Po grounds. The male and female masseurs certainly know what they are doing, and although it looks (and sometimes feels) a little painful to be pulled into all those weird positions, the after-effect is heavenly.
✚ B/C9 ✉ Wat Po, Thanon Maha Rat ☎ 222 0933 ⊙ Daily 8–6 🚍 A/C bus 6, 7, 8, 12, 44 ⛴ Tian pier 💷 200B per hour, 120B per half-hour, or 300B for an hour with herbs

VEJAKORN

High-quality massages in peaceful surroundings. Very good value.
✚ G11 ✉ Surawong Plaza, Thanon Surawong ☎ 237 5576 ⊙ Daily 10AM–midnight 🚍 A/C bus 2, 7 💷 260B for two hours

MURALS

BUDDHAISAWAN CHAPEL
The exceptionally fine 18th-century murals of this chapel form one of the highlights of a visit to the National Museum.

🚩 B7/8 ⊠ National Museum, Thanon Naphratad ☎ 224 1333 🕐 Wed –Sun 9 – 4 🍴 Cafeteria 🚌 A/C bus 3, 6, 7, 39 🚢 Maha Rat pier ♿ Few 💲 Cheap

WAT BOWON NIWET
Peaceful *wat* to wander around, with some unusual murals clearly depicting foreigners in Thailand. There are scenes of Englishmen at the races and American missionaries getting off a boat.

🚩 C7 ⊠ Thanon Phra Sumen 🕐 Daily 8 –5 🍴 Street stalls and the Vijit restaurant (► 63) 🚌 A/C bus 11 💲 Free

WAT PATHUM WANARAM
The murals at this peaceful *wat* are interesting for their clear Western influence. Western culture introduced a third dimension to the traditional two-dimensional Thai mural paintings, making them more comprehensible to our eyes. Note the lovely scenes depicting a procession of royal barges.

🚩 G9 ⊠ Thanon Rama I 🕐 Daily 9 –5 🚌 A/C bus 1, 8, 11, 13 💲 Free

WAT SUWANNARAM
Art historians consider the recently restored murals in this elegant *wat* (attributed to the foremost painters of King Rama III's reign) amongst the city's finest.

🚩 A7 ⊠ Klong Bangkok Noi 🕐 Daily 🚌 A/C bus 7, 9, 10 🚢 Bangkok Noi canal taxi from Maha Rat pier 💲 Free

WAT THONG NOPPAKUM
Early Bangkok temple, built during the reign of King Rama IV, with well-preserved mural paintings.

🚩 D10 ⊠ Near the river on Soi Wat Thong, off Thanon Somdet Chao Phraya 🕐 Daily 8 –5 🚢 Cross-river ferry from Song Sawat pier to Wat Thong pier 💲 Free

WAT THONG THAMMACHAT
Temple from the Ayutthaya period with murals depicting daily life in old Bangkok.

🚩 D10 ⊠ Near Wat Thong pier 🕐 Daily 8 –5 🚢 Cross-river ferry from Song Sawat pier to Wat Thong pier 💲 Free

Thai mural painting

The subject of murals is repeated in most temples. On the walls facing and behind the main Buddha image are scenes from Buddha's life, while the side walls show Jataka paintings (scenes from his previous lives). Most interesting for Western visitors are often the lower parts of the walls, with scenes depicting daily life in Thailand. Because of the climate and the materials used, murals rarely last, and it is hard to find any dating back more than 150 or 200 years.

Wat Suwannaram

CANALS

Getting lost

There is no proper map available of the Thonburi klongs. According to Bangkok-based author William Warren, a foreigner who asked for one from the government was told that such information was a 'military secret'. In fact, you don't really need one as there are hardly any major sights along the way and getting lost is all part of the fun.

Live the *klong* life

East West Siam (☎ 256 6669; fax 256 7166; ➤ 19, panel) organises alternative *klong* tours and offers the chance of staying overnight in a small *klong* house with six simple guest rooms. This is a unique opportunity to share the life led by most Thais and to understand something of their culture and traditions.

Traditional klong life, with houses built on stilts

See Top 25 Sights for
CHAO PHRAYA RIVER (➤ 28)
KLONG BANGKOK YAI (➤ 25)
See Travel Facts (➤ 90)

DAMNOEN SADUAK FLOATING MARKET

This lively floating market (*talaat naam*), is slowly being invaded by tour groups, but still has character. Talaat Ton Khem is the main market, but most tourists aim for the Talaat Hia Kui, which has long-tail boats laden with souvenirs. On a side canal is the most authentic of the three markets, Talaat Khun Phitak, which can be reached by water-taxi.
✚ Off map at A13 ✉ Klong Damnoen Saduak, Ratchaburi Province, 104km south-west of Bangkok ⏱ 5–10AM 🍴 Foodstalls on boats
🚌 Early bus 78 from Bangkok's Southern Bus Terminal, leaving every 20 minutes from 6AM, then take a water-taxi from the pier near the bus station or walk along the canal to the market

KLONG BANGKOK NOI

Once you have passed the Royal Barge Museum (➤ 24) and the little-visited Wat Suwannaram (➤ 57), there is a touch of the jungle between old crumbling *wats* and typical Thai teak houses.
✚ A–B7 🚤 Cheap canal taxis go up the *klong* from Maha Rat pier, and long-tail boats leave from Chang Wang Luang pier. Private companies operate excursions to the Royal Barge Museum and further up the *klong* from Chang Wang Luang pier

KLONG OM

Wonderful excursion through durian plantations, fruit orchards, little temples and grand river mansions. Recommended for a feel of rural Thailand.
✚ Off map at C1 ✉ Nonthaburi 🍴 Floating restaurant at the end of Nonthaburi promenade 🚤 Chao Phraya express boat north to the last stop (Nonthaburi pier), then long-tail boat up Klong Om

KLONG SAN SAP

The fastest way to get across one of the most congested parts of the city, and undoubtedly the most adventurous and exotic. The urban *klong* scenery is an eye-opener, but the stench of the water can be quite overwhelming.
✚ D8–J9 ✉ From Golden Mount parallel to Thanon Bamrung Muang, Thanon Rama I, Thanon Ploenchit and Thanon Sukhumwit 🚤 Long-tail boats operate eastwards from Phanfa pier at the Golden Mount, past Jim Thompson's House, with useful stops at Thanon Phaya Thai, Prathunam, Thanon Witthayu (Wireless Road) and Sukhumwit Soi 23

FESTIVALS

See What's On (► 22)

ASALHA PUJA

This is the third most important Buddhist holiday, marking the day of Lord Buddha's first sermon. Thais gather at temples in the evening waiting for the moon to rise, then they follow the chanting monks three times around the *wat*, carrying flowers, incense and candles which they then offer in front of the temple.

KITE FIGHTS

During breezy afternoons in March and April, Sanam Luang turns into a colourful spectacle of magnificent kites. The huge 'male' kites, or *chulas*, try to catch the smaller 'females', or *pukpaos*, to the cheers of the public.

LOY KRATHONG

According to legend, a princess in Sukhothai made a small boat from a banana leaf to please her king; this has since become a rite of thanks to Mae Khongkha (Mother of Waters). On the night of the full moon in November, at the time of the floods, rivers and *klongs* are lit up with thousands of floating candles and riverside hotels organise special parties.

MAGA PUJA

In commemoration of the day 1,200 disciples gathered to hear Buddha preach, Thais go to *wats* to listen to sermons by the chief monk. When the moon rises they circle the *wat* as during Asalha Puja.

SONGKRAN

The water-throwing festival is the chance for every normally very reserved Thai to let loose. Some water is sprinkled on friends to bless them, but strangers often get more than that. Expect to be completely soaked by midday, but who cares in the heat of April?

VISAKA PUJA

The holiest day of the Buddhist year is the day Lord Buddha was born, became enlightened and died. This is one of the more public holidays and ends with a candle-lit procession around *wats*. It is at its most solemn in Wat Benjamaborpit (► 50).

High spirits at the annual Songkran water-throwing festival, held in April

Three-month retreat

Tradition has it that farmers asked Buddha to keep all the monks in their *wats* for the three months after they planted out their rice, because otherwise the monks walked all over the young shoots when collecting their morning alms. Buddha took them seriously and there is still a three-month retreat period for monks (Khao Pansa), which starts with Asalha Puja and ends in October when people go to *wats* with new robes for the monks.

ATTRACTIONS FOR CHILDREN

See Top 25 Sights for
BOAT RIDES ON THE CHAO PHRAYA RIVER
(► 28)
KITE FLYING IN SANAM LUANG (► 32)
ROWING IN LUMPHINI PARK (► 45)
TURTLES IN WAT PRAYOON (► 34)

Cooling down

Most moderate and up-market hotels have swimming pools to cool you down, but not all are suitable for children. The best pools for youngsters are at the Shangri-La and the Marriott Royal Garden Riverside (► 84). Siam Water Park is a fantastic place with pools and waterslides ⊠ 101 Sukhaphiban 2, Minburi, 10km north-east of Bangkok ☎ 517 0075 ▣ Non-AC bus 26 or 27 from Victory Monument.

ADVENTURELAND

An 18-hole mini golf course, a roller coaster, a moving cinema and a roller-blade rink are just a few of the attractions.

⊞ Off map ⊠ Seacon Square, 904 Thanon Srinakin ☎ 721 8888/96 ⏰ Mon–Fri 11–9; Sat–Sun 10–10 ⛱ Free; coupons 15–30B ▣ Microbus 15

DUSIT ZOO (KHAO DIN WANA)

Includes rare species such as the Komodo dragon, and the royal white elephants, sadly chained for most of the time (a new and larger elephant enclosure is planned). Children can ride elephants or rent a paddle-boat, and a circus is held at weekends 11AM–2PM.
⊞ E6 ⊠ Thanon Rama V and Thanon Ratchawithi ☎ 281 0000 ⏰ Daily 8–6 🍴 Two lakeside Thai restaurants ▣ A/C bus 10, 16 ♿ Good ⛱ Cheap

MAGIC LAND (DAN NERAMIT)

A mini version of Disneyland, with animated dinosaurs, ferris wheels and a ghost house.
⊞ H4 ⊠ 72 Thanon Pahonyotin, near Central Plaza ☎ 513 1731 ⏰ Mon–Fri 10–5:30; Sat–Sun 10–7 ⛱ Moderate ▣ A/C bus 2, 3, 9, 10, 13, 14, 29, 39

MUSEUM OF IMAGING TECHNOLOGY

Excellent hi-tech museum of photography with several interactive rooms for kids.
⊞ G10 ⊠ Chulalongkorn University, Thanon Phaya Thai ⏰ Sat and Sun 10–4 ▣ A/C bus 1, 2, 29 ♿ Few ⛱ Moderate

RED CROSS (PASTEUR INSTITUTE) SNAKE FARM

Wide display of poisonous snakes, plus demonstrations of snake handling and venom milking.
⊞ G10 ⊠ Thanon Rama IV and Thanon Henri Dunant ☎ 252 0161 ⏰ Daily 8:30–4:30. Snake-handling demonstrations weekdays 10:30, 2; weekends and holidays 10:30 ▣ A/C bus 2, 7 ♿ None ⛱ Moderate

SAFARI WORLD

Incorporates a 7km-drive past giraffes, lions, rhinos and monkeys, a marine park and an amazing bird area.
⊞ Off map at K1 ⊠ 9km from the city centre in Minburi ☎ 518 1000 ⏰ Mon–Sun 9–4:30 ⛱ 400B for adults, 300B for children ▣ 26 from Victory Monument to Minburi

Up, up and away in Sanam Luang

BANGKOK
where to...

GOURMET THAI

Prices

Approximate prices for a meal for two excluding drinks:

£ = under 400B

££ = under 1,000B

£££ = over 1,000B

A typical Thai meal

Most Thai gourmet restaurants offer a set menu, which may be a good option if you are trying Thai food for the first time. Thais often start with drinks and some small snacks or a spicy salad, followed by several main courses set in the middle of the table: usually at least a curry, a noodle dish, steamed rice and a soup. Thais eat with a spoon (right hand), using a fork (left hand) to help food on to the spoon. They take just one spoonful of a dish so as not to appear greedy, and then move on to the next one.

Taking it home

Recipes from the beautiful Celadon restaurant at the Sukhothai Hotel have been collected and published as *The Food of Thailand* (Periplus Editions, 1995).

BAAN KHANITHA (££–£££)

Up-market Thai restaurant in a stylish house, offering exceptionally well-prepared creative Thai dishes, though the mobile phones of yuppie clients can be somewhat off-putting.

➕ Off map at K9/10 ✉ 36/1 Sukhumwit Soi 23 (Soi Prasanmit) ☎ 258 4181 🕐 Lunch, dinner 🚌 A/C bus 1, 8, 11, 13

BAN CHIANG (££)

With an exceptional address, this intimate restaurant is housed in an old Thai house tucked away between sky-scrapers, and is furnished with antiques. It serves a large choice of delicious traditional Thai dishes. Highly recommended.

➕ F12 ✉ 14 Thanon Srivieng, off Thanon Silom ☎ 236 7045 🕐 Lunch, dinner 🚌 A/C bus 2, 4, 5, 15

BUSSARACUM (££)

Traditional favourite for its royal Thai cuisine and classical, elegant décor. Minced pork and shrimp in egg-net wrapping was supposedly King Rama II's preferred appetiser, and if it was good enough for him...

➕ G11 ✉ 35 Soi Phiphat 2, off Thanon Convent ☎ 235 8915 🕐 Lunch, dinner 🚌 A/C bus 2, 4, 5, 15

CELADON (££–£££)

One of Bangkok's most beautiful restaurants: inside it's minimalist Thai, outside there are lotus ponds and banana trees. The modern Thai cuisine is just as spectacular, the roast duck curry being particularly good. For newcomers there are two extensive set menus. Highly recommended.

➕ H11 ✉ Sukhothai Hotel, 13/3 Thanon Satorn Tai ☎ 287 0222 ext 5722 🕐 Lunch, dinner 🚌 A/C bus 5

ONCE UPON A TIME (££)

Refined Thai food in elegant, authentic Thai surroundings with lots of teak, antiques and old Thai music. Try the 'fish of the 7th day', a speciality of the north-east, or the wonderful tamarind soup.

➕ G/H8 ✉ 7th Floor, Juldis Tower (opposite First House), Soi Phetburi 19 ☎ 255 4948 🕐 Lunch, dinner 🚌 A/C bus 5, 11

SALATHIP (£££)

Carefully prepared royal Thai cuisine in the romantic and elegant setting of a carved teak pavilion that overlooks the Chao Phraya river and lotus ponds.

➕ E11 ✉ Riverside, Shangri-La Hotel, 8 Soi Wat Suan Phu ☎ 236 7777 ext 1168 🕐 Nightly 6:30–11 🚌 A/C bus 4, 15 🚢 Oriental or Shangri-La piers

THE SPICE MARKET (££–£££)

One of the city's finest Thai restaurants, with a décor that re-creates an old shophouse filled with spice sacks and jars. The food is simply delicious, while the special herbal drinks on offer claim to provide longevity or an adventurous sex life.

➕ H9 ✉ Regent Hotel, 155 Thanon Ratchadamri ☎ 251 6127 🕐 Lunch, dinner 🚌 A/C bus 4, 5, 15

Standard Thai

CABBAGES AND CONDOMS (£–££)

Unusual restaurant with excellent Thai classic cooking, also serving up information on birth control and Aids as it is affiliated to the Population Development Association.

✚ K10 ✉ 10 Sukhumwit Soi 12 ☎ 251 5552 🕐 Daily 11–10 🚌 A/C bus 1, 8, 11, 13

D'JIT POCHANA (£–££)

Thailand's best-known chain of restaurants; this one serves good, standard Thai dishes in an uninspiring room. Excellent-value lunch buffet with Thai and Chinese dishes. The airport branch at 23/368–380 Thanon Panolyotin (☎ 531 2716) is convenient for delayed travellers, and there is another branch at 60 Sukhumwit Soi 20 (☎ 258 1578).

✚ K2 ✉ 1082 Thanon Phahonyothin, near Chatuchak Weekend Market ☎ 279 5000 🕐 Lunch, dinner 🚌 A/C bus 2, 3, 9, 10, 12, 13, 29, 39

KALOANG HOME KITCHEN (£)

Very Thai-style restaurant serving inventive Thai dishes on a covered pier and old boat near the Royal Yacht Pier. Trust the daily specials. Recommended.

✚ C6 ✉ 2 Thanon Sri Ayudhaya, overlooking the Chao Phraya river ☎ 281 9228 🕐 Daily 11–11 🚌 A/C bus 5, 6 ⛴ Thewet pier

LEMON GRASS (££)

This palm-shaded townhouse with a distinctive Asian interior is an old favourite, and serves delicious and imaginative Thai dishes with a touch of 'royalty'. Worth a try on your first night as they are used to catering for resident *farangs* (foreigners)!

✚ Off map at K10 ✉ 5/1 Sukhumwit Soi 24 ☎ 258 8637 🕐 Lunch, dinner 🚌 A/C bus 1, 8, 11, 13

THE MANGO TREE (££)

Regional Thai cooking in an old Siamese house or in its garden under the mango tree. Live traditional Thai music accompanies the not-too-spicy food. Good for beginners.

✚ G11 ✉ 37 Soi Annubahn Rajdhon, off Thanon Surawong opposite Tawana Ramada Hotel ☎ 236 2820 🕐 Lunch, dinner 🚌 A/C bus 2, 4, 5, 15

SEVEN SEAS (££)

Trendy hang-out for Bangkok's young and avant-garde crowd, serving very good 'nouvelle' Thai cuisine.

✚ Off map at K10 ✉ Sukhumwit Soi 33 ☎ 259 7662 🕐 Lunch, dinner 🚌 A/C bus 1, 8, 11, 13

VIJIT (£–££)

An old-school Bangkok restaurant with a cafeteria atmosphere and excellent, unpretentious food.

✚ C/D8 ✉ 77/2 Thanon Ratchadamnoen Klang ☎ 281 6472 🕐 Lunch, dinner 🚌 A/C bus 3, 6, 9, 11, 12, 39, 44

Delightful fruits

Fruit is important in the Thai diet and is plentiful all year round. You can buy it from the market and can trust it ready-cut from street stalls.

• All year round: pomelo (big grapefruit), tangerine, guava, a variety of bananas, papaya, coconut, watermelon, sapodilla (tastes like fresh figs), and tasty pineapples, grapes and apples.

• Seasonal: rambutan, mangosteen, durian (pungent odour), rose apples, mangoes, lychees, green plums and strawberries.

THAI FOOD & CULTURE

Food culture

If you become addicted to delicious Thai food, why not try a cookery class? The Thai Cooking School at the Oriental Hotel (➤ 39 ☎ 238 0265) organises a course of five morning classes (you can attend just one if you prefer), dedicated to the preparation of Thai dishes and to the culture that surrounds it. The Dusit Thani Hotel (➤ 84 ☎ 236 6400), the UFM Baking and Cooking School (✉ Sukhumwit Soi 33 ☎ 259 0620) and the Modern Women Institute (✉ 45/6–7 Thanon Set Siri ☎ 279 2831/4) all organise short Thai cookery classes.

BAAN THAI (££)

Excellent Thai cuisine accompanied by classical Thai dancing 7:30–10PM.

➕ Off map at K10
✉ 7 Sukhumwit Soi 32 ☎ 258 5403 🕐 Dinner 7–11 🚌 A/C bus 1, 8, 11, 13

MANOHRA (£££)

Authentic Thai dinner served on board a 40-year-old rice barge, cruising past the illuminated Wat Arun and Grand Palace. More peaceful and luxurious atmosphere than that found aboard most cruise boats.

➕ Just off map at C13
✉ Marriott Royal Garden Riverside, 257/1–3 Thanon Charoen Nakorn (at Krung Thep Bridge) ☎ 476 0021/2 ext 1406 🕐 Departs every evening from the hotel's pier at 7:30, returning at 10 🚤 Free shuttle boat from Oriental Hotel and River City Shopping Complex

SALA RIM NAAM (£££)

Another Bangkok institution, the Rim Naam has a wonderful atmosphere and stages daily performances by dancers from the Fine Arts School. The food itself sometimes takes second place to the spectacle.

➕ E11 ✉ Thonburi side of the Oriental Hotel (48 Soi Oriental) ☎ 437 6211 🕐 Lunch, dinner (Thai dance at 8:30PM) 🚌 A/C bus 4, 15 🚤 Free boat from the hotel's pier

SALA SABAI RIVER NIGHTMARKET (£££)

Splendid dinner buffet with seafood, grills and Thai favourites served from colourful market stalls overlooking the great river. Daily traditional Thai music and dance performances.

➕ E11 ✉ Royal Orchid Sheraton, 2 Soi Captain Bush, Thanon Sri Phraya ☎ 266 0123 🕐 Daily, dinner 7–10 🚌 Non-A/C bus 36, 93 🚤 Sri Phraya pier

SILOM VILLAGE (££)

Huge semi-outdoor restaurant surrounded by craft and textile shops. Wide selection of fresh seafood to choose from, as well as other Thai dishes. Friendly family-style atmosphere (children welcome), with a good show every night of traditional Thai dances and music. Recommended.

➕ F11 ✉ 286 Thanon Silom ☎ 234 4448 🕐 10AM–11PM 🚌 A/C bus 2, 4, 5, 15

TUMNAK THAI (££)

Claims to be the world's largest restaurant, a village with pavilions offering food from every region in Thailand. Traditional dancing, waiters on roller-skates...it could only happen in Bangkok.

➕ Off map at K1
✉ 131 Thanon Ratchadaphisek ☎ 274 6420 🕐 Daily 11–11 🚌 A/C bus 15, 18, 22

WAN FAH (££)

Pleasant evening cruise on the river with Thai or seafood set menu and classical Thai music.

➕ E11 ✉ Leaves from River City pier; reservations 12/14 River City Shopping Complex ☎ 433 5453 🕐 Daily 7–9PM 🚌 Non-A/C bus 1, 35, 36, 75, 93 🚤 Sri Phraya pier

SEAFOOD

LORD JIM (£££)

Lord Jim is a uniquely stylish riverside room, where Californian, Thai, Indian and Japanese chefs do wonderful things with seafood. The lunch buffet is still a city institution. There is also a *sushi* bar, a small oyster bar, a cocktail bar and live music nightly. Another bonus is the good views over the Chao Phraya river.

✚ E11 ✉ Oriental Hotel, 48 Soi Oriental ☎ 236 0400 🕐 Lunch, dinner 🚌 Non-A/C bus 1, 35, 75 ⛴ Oriental pier

SAVOEY SEAFOOD (££–£££)

Popular with Chinese businessmen for the *dim sum* lunch, but over 500 Chinese dishes are served in the restaurant (built like a wooden boat) or on the cool terrace overlooking the river. And if this isn't enough, there is a large variety of vegetables, fresh fish and seafood to choose from and many different ways of having it cooked.

✚ E11 ✉ River Bank Verandah, River City Shopping Complex, Soi Captain Bush ☎ 237 7557/8 ext 120/126 🕐 Lunch, dinner 🚌 A/C Microbus 6, 7 ⛴ Sri Phraya pier

SEAFOOD MARKET (££–£££)

This restaurant's slogan is: 'If it swims we have it!' And there is more: an unbelievable selection of the freshest seafood, vegetables and fruit, all sold by weight and prepared in the style of your choosing, or as your food consultant (these are more than mere waiters) recommends.

✚ K10 ✉ 85 Sukhumvit Soi 24 ☎ 261 2071 🕐 11AM–midnight 🚌 A/C bus 1, 8, 11, 13

SOMBOON SEAFOOD (££)

Extremely popular and moderately priced seafood restaurant, usually crowded with Thai families. The décor is no-nonsense but the crab curry is known as one of the best in town.

✚ G11 ✉ Thanon Surawong, near the Montien Hotel 🕐 Lunch, dinner until midnight 🚌 A/C bus 2, 7

WIT'S OYSTER BAR AND RESTAURANT (££–£££)

One of the city's few oyster bars, re-creating the atmosphere of London's Wheeler's Restaurant, with fresh oysters, fish and chips and other British dishes.

✚ J9 ✉ 20/10–11 Soi Ruam Ruedi, off Thanon Ploenchit ☎ 251 9455 🕐 11:30AM–11:30PM 🚌 A/C bus 1, 8

YOK YOR (££)

Popular Thai-style seafood restaurant on the banks of the Chao Phraya, with Thai, Chinese, Japanese and European dishes and live pop music. The speciality is a fiery *haw mok*, or fish curry. An inexpensive evening cruise leaves daily at 8PM.

✚ C6 ✉ 4 Thanon Wisut Kasat ☎ 280 1418 🕐 10AM–11:30PM 🚌 A/C bus 6 ⛴ Wisuthi pier

The love of food

Thais love eating, as is obvious from the wide selection of restaurants in Bangkok – it is claimed that there are over 50,000, and that's not counting the foodstalls that set up on every street and the food boats along the canals. You won't go hungry, that's for sure. But if your heart is set on one particular restaurant, be sure to book in advance – others might feel the same way about it.

ALL ASIAN

Chinese cuisine

If you want to cool your palate down after the often fiery Thai food, try one of the more authentic Chinese restaurants. Most Chinese in Bangkok come from the Guangdong and Yunnan provinces, well known for their delicious cuisine. Some of the best food can be sampled at the hundreds of cheap street stalls in Chinatown, or in the more expensive Chinese restaurants in hotels – there are very few Chinese restaurants in the middle price range.

CHINESE

CHINA HOUSE (£££)

The best of classic Cantonese and regional Chinese cuisine served in an elegant, beautifully restored private residence outside the Oriental Hotel. *Dim sum* is available at lunchtime.

✚ E11 ✉ Oriental Hotel, 48 Soi Oriental ☎ 236 0400 ⓘ Lunch, dinner 🚌 Non-A/C bus 1, 35, 75 ⛴ Oriental pier

HOI THIEN LAO RIM NAM (££–£££)

One of the oldest and finest of Bangkok's Chinese restaurants has moved from Chinatown to Thonburi. Its specialities are shark's-fin soup and steamed grouper.

✚ C11 ✉ 1449, 1 Thanon Latya, Thonburi (opposite River City Shopping Complex) ☎ 434 1121 ⓘ Lunch, dinner 🚌 A/C bus 5, 6, 10

SHANGARILA (££)

Over-the-top and very glitzy Chinese restaurant which, surprisingly, serves quite inexpensive but imaginative Shanghai-style dishes. The place is extremely popular and reservations are a must, especially at night.

✚ G11 ✉ 154/4–5 Thanon Silom, near Thanon Rama IV ☎ 234 0861 ⓘ Daily 11–10 🚌 A/C bus 2, 4, 5, 15

SIANG PING LOH (£££)

Grand new restaurant in the heart of Chinatown. Join the local businessmen for more-than-excellent *dim sum* (lunch only) or try the mouthwatering Cantonese and Szechuan specialities.

✚ D9 ✉ 8th floor, Grand China Princess Hotel, 215 Thanon Yaowarat, corner of Thanon Ratchawong ☎ 224 9977 ⓘ Lunch, dinner 🚌 A/C bus 1, 7 ⛴ Ratchawong pier

INDIAN

HIMALI CHA CHA (££)

Cha Cha started off as cook to Lord Mountbatten in India, then to Indian ambassadors around the world, before he and his family settled in Bangkok. Specialities include Mughal Muslim, vegetarian and northern Indian dishes, all served in a charming if old-fashioned Indian décor. Long-time favourite with expats and tourists alike.

✚ E11 ✉ 1229/11 Thanon Charoen Krung (New Road), corner of Thanon Surawong ☎ 235 1569 ⓘ Lunch, dinner 🚌 A/C bus 2, 4, 5, 15 ⛴ Oriental pier

MRS BALBIR'S (££)

This restaurant is run by an Indian from Malaysia, and is very popular for its north Indian food and delicious chicken dishes. If you get hooked, join one of the cookery classes run by Mrs Balbir.

✚ J9 ✉ 155/18 Sukhumwit Soi 11 ☎ 253 2281 ⓘ Lunch, dinner 🚌 A/C bus 1, 8, 11, 13

RANG MAHAL (££)

Some of the finest Indian food in town served in a pleasant and elegant décor, and accompanied by Indian classical music.

✚ Off map at K10 ✉ Rooftop of the Rembrandt Hotel, Sukhumwit Soi 18 ☎ 261 7100 ⓘ Lunch, dinner 🚌 A/C bus 1, 8, 11, 13

ROYAL INDIA RESTAURANT (£)

Another delightful but hard-to-find place (squeezed between Chinatown and Phahurat), which is renowned for its well-prepared North Indian cuisine. Vegetarians will find a larger selection of vegetable dishes here than in most other Bangkok restaurants.

✚ C/D9 ✉ 392/1 Thanon Chakpetch – small *soi* south of Soi Wanit 1 (Sampeng Lane) ☎ 221 6565 ◷ Daily 10–10 🚍 A/C bus 1, 7

JAPANESE

BENIHANA (££)

A meal in the Benihana is a show, your table being the stage on which chefs skilled in the ancient art of *hibachi* cooking perform: chop, chop, stir and slice, for your eyes only.

✚ Off map at B/C13 ✉ Marriott Royal Garden Riverside, Thanon Charoen Nakorn ☎ 476 0021 ext 1442 ◷ Lunch, dinner 🚢 Free shuttle boat from the River City Shopping Complex and Oriental Hotel

GENJI (£££)

A peaceful restaurant overlooking lush landscaped gardens, and offering a mouthwatering selection of the best in Japanese cuisine. *Sushi, makisushi, sashimi,* grills, noodles and hotpots – you name it, it's here, and prepared with great skill. Recommended and very popular with Japanese expats.

✚ H9 ✉ Hilton International, 2 Thanon Witthayu (Wireless Road) ☎ 253 0123 ◷ Lunch, dinner 🚍 A/C bus 12

VIETNAMESE

LE DALAT (££)

Delightful restaurant in another stylish ex-residence, with a beautifully landscaped garden. The divinely prepared food is Vietnamese with an unmistakable touch of French. The house specialities are reason enough to return again and again.

✚ Off map at K10 ✉ 47/1 Sukhumwit Soi 23 ☎ 258 4192 ◷ Lunch, dinner 🚍 A/C bus 1, 8, 11, 13

MADAME CHERIE'S KITCHEN (£–££)

One of the oldest Vietnamese restaurants in town, serving authentic, good-value Vietnamese specialities as well as a few Thai and international dishes. Very quick and welcoming service.

✚ H11 ✉ 1st floor, Charn Issara Tower, Thanon Rama IV ☎ 237 1729 ◷ 11ᴀᴍ–10ᴘᴍ 🚍 A/C bus 7

PHO (££–£££)

A trendy restaurant serving some of the best Vietnamese cuisine in town. Has a modern décor with no frills.

✚ K10 ✉ 3rd floor, Sukhumwit Plaza, Sukhumwit Soi 12 ☎ 252 5601 ◷ Lunch, dinner 🚍 A/C bus 1, 8, 11, 13

Vegetarian options

Vegetarians who visit Bangkok during the annual Vegetarian Festival (September–October) will find Chinatown awash with foodstalls serving Thai and Chinese vegetarian dishes. At other times of the year a choice of fresh vegetable dishes is served at most Indian and Thai restaurants. The city's best vegetarian restaurant is The Whole Earth (✉ 93/3 Soi Lang Suan, off Thanon Ploenchit ☎ 252 5574). Try also Vegeta (✉ 6th floor, Isetan, World Trade Center, Thanon Ratchadamri ☎ 255 9569), which specialises in mock meat dishes, or the Vegetarian Bangkok Society (☎ 656 8300), which meets on the first and third Wednesday of each month.

ALL WESTERN

High tea

Chinese claim that hot tea is the best way to cool down and to recover from the heat, and surely the English will not disapprove. The traditional place to take tea in Bangkok is the Author's Lounge in the Oriental Hotel, but the grand lobbies of the Hilton International and Regent (➤ 84), and the Grand Hyatt Erawan (✉ 494 Thanon Ratchadamri ☎ 254 1234) and Shangri-La (✉ 89 Soi Wat Suan Plu ☎ 236 7777) also offer splendid teatime buffets of pastries, sandwiches, Thai sweets, pies and scones, accompanied by uplifting classical music.

AMERICAN

BOURBON STREET (££)

Charming Cajun restaurant with New Orleans/ Southern-style specials such as jambalaya, blackened red fish and pecan pie. Also has an American-style bar.

✚ Off map at K10 ✉ 29/4–6 Washington Square, Sukhumwit Soi 22 ☎ 259 0328/9 🕐 Daily 7AM–1AM 🚌 A/C bus 1, 8, 11, 13

NEIL'S TAVERN (£££)

Any homesick American will feel in his element at Neil's, which specialises in American-style seafood and beef imported from the States. Lunch tends to be quite formal as the restaurant is popular with staff from the nearby embassies, while dinner is a more relaxed affair.

✚ J9 ✉ 58/4 Soi Ruam Ruedi, off Thanon Ploenchit ☎ 256 6874 🕐 Mon–Sat lunch, dinner; Sun dinner only 🚌 A/C bus 1, 8, 11, 13

PLANET HOLLYWOOD (££)

Huge burger portions (both meat and veggie), cocktails and good fries, all served with live music from 10PM onwards. On the 15th of each month there is a major film screening.

✚ H9 ✉ Gaysorn Plaza, Thanon Gesorn, off Thanon Ploenchit ☎ 656 1358 🕐 Daily 11AM–2AM 🚌 A/C bus 1, 8, 11, 13

BRITISH

CUMBRIAN (££)

The Cumbrian has a small menu offering British dishes such as sausages (six different types) with mash and steak and kidney pies. In addition, it has a large range of local and imported beers.

✚ H11 ✉ 120/1 Saladaeng Soi 1 ☎ 233 4074 🕐 Daily 11–11 🚌 A/C bus 1, 8, 11, 13

CONTINENTAL

KANIT RESTAURANT (£–££)

Casual restaurant with well-prepared Mediterranean specialities such as pastas, pizzas and steaks, all served with a touch of the Orient.

✚ C8 ✉ 68 Thanon Titong, near Wat Suthat ☎ 222 4936 🕐 Mon–Sat 11–11 🚌 A/C bus 8

THE REGENT GRILL (£££)

The Regent Grill has an inventive Californian-style menu, often combining the best of Mediterranean and Asian cuisines. The set-menu lunch is reasonably priced but very popular. Dinner tends to be more expensive, but is worth the extra. Even the décor blends Western and Eastern elements.

✚ H9 ✉ Regent Hotel, 155 Thanon Ratchadamri ☎ 251 6127 🕐 Mon–Fri lunch, dinner; Sat–Sun dinner only 🚌 A/C bus 4, 5, 15

FRENCH

LE BANYAN (££–£££)

Atmospheric French restaurant in an old Bangkok house decorated with local furnishings and objets d'art. The house speciality is a traditional pressed duck (for two), and many dishes show Thai influences.

➕ J10 ✉ 59 Sukhumwit Soi 8 ☎ 253 5556 🕐 Lunch Mon–Fri 12–2, 7–10; Sat 7–10 🚌 A/C bus 1, 8, 11, 13

LE BISTROT (££–£££)

Excellent, rather classic French food and a pleasant atmosphere; popular with staff from the nearby embassies.

➕ J9 ✉ 20/17–19 Soi Ruam Ruedi, off Thanon Ploenchit ☎ 251 2523 🕐 Mon–Fri 11:30–2:30, 6:30–11; Sat–Sun 6:30–11 🚌 A/C bus 1, 8, 11, 13

LE BOUCHON (££)

This cosy French bistro, a favourite among Bangkok's French expat community and set in pleasant surroundings, has simple but delicious French food prepared by a French chef from Lyon.

➕ G11 ✉ 37/17 Patpong Soi 2 ☎ 234 9109 🕐 Daily 6PM–midnight 🚌 A/C bus 2, 4, 5, 15

DIVA (££–£££)

This excellent French restaurant, very popular with what is left of Bangkok's yuppies, has attentive service and elegant surroundings. Recommended, so book in advance.

➕ Off map at K10 ✉ 49 Sukhumwit Soi 49 ☎ 258 7879 🕐 Lunch, dinner 🚌 A/C bus 1, 8, 11, 13

LE NORMANDIE (£££)

For a formal, definitively elegant dining experience, come to the Normandie (if you have a reservation). A wide choice of exquisite à la carte dishes, a good-value *menu dégustation*, impeccable service and stunning panoramic river views.

➕ E11 ✉ Top floor of Oriental Hotel, 48 Soi Oriental ☎ 236 0400 🕐 Lunch, dinner 🚌 A/C bus 1, 35, 75 ⛴ Oriental pier

ITALIAN

ANGELINI (££–£££)

This stunning Italian restaurant, set over three floors, has become one of Bangkok's places to be seen. The food is traditional Italian from several regions, and the live band at night draws the crowds. Very lively atmosphere.

➕ E11 ✉ Shangri-La, 89 Soi Wat Suan Plu, off Thanon Charoen Krung ☎ 236 7777 🕐 Breakfast, lunch, dinner 🚌 A/C bus 2 ⛴ Shangri-La pier

PAN PAN L'OSTERIA (££)

Popular Italian trattoria with good pasta and pizza, plus the best home-made *gelati* in town.

➕ Off map at K10 ✉ 6–6/1 Sukhumwit Soi 33 ☎ 258 9304 🕐 10AM–11PM 🚌 A/C bus 1, 8, 11, 13

VITO'S (££–£££)

Classic Italian food in a typical, somewhat old-fashioned room. Excellent buffet of antipasti and the biggest selection of *grappas* in Thailand.

➕ J9 ✉ 20/2–3 Soi Ruam Ruedi, off Thanon Ploenchit ☎ 251 9455 🕐 Mon–Fri 11:30–2:30, 6–11; Sat–Sun 6–11 🚌 A/C bus 1, 8, 11, 13

Good-value buffets

The best Western food is to be found at hotels, but it tends to be expensive. Travellers on a tighter budget should instead check out the better-value lunch and dinner buffets. Sunday brunch (11–3) at the Sukhothai Hotel's Colonnade Restaurant, to the accompaniment of a jazz combo, is an absolute favourite with expats (➤ 84; book well in advance). Le Meridien President (✉ 971 Thanon Ploenchit ☎ 253 0444) has a popular lunch and dinner buffet with both Thai and French or Italian dishes. The Oriental Hotel's alfresco buffet is more expensive, but the riverside setting alone makes it worth while (➤ 39).

ANTIQUES

Thai customs and antiques

Fakes are particularly well made in Thailand and are sometimes sold as genuine antiques. To protect yourself, buy from a reputable shop. Antiques and Buddha images cannot be exported without a licence, which can be obtained from the Fine Arts Department at the National Museum (✉ Thanon Naphratad ☎ 221 4817). Some antique shops will arrange the paperwork for you. Applications, submitted with two photographs of the object and a photocopy of your passport, usually take about five days to be processed.

L'ARCADIA

A small shop with well-priced antique furniture and carved teak architectural ornaments, mainly from Thailand and Myanmar (Burma).
⊞ Off map at K10 ✉ 12/2 Sukhumvit Soi 23 ☎ 259 9595 🚍 A/C bus 1, 8, 11, 13

THE FINE ARTS

Small but very stylish collection of Buddhist statues, terracotta objects and fine antique fabrics from all over the region, as well as terracotta reproductions of the Sukhothai art pieces that were used to decorate this elegant hotel.
⊞ H11 ✉ Shop no 4, Sukhothai Hotel, 13/3 Thanon Satorn Tai ☎ 287 0222 🕐 Daily 10–6 🚍 A/C bus 5

THE GOLDEN TRIANGLE

One of the best shops for old hill-tribe artefacts, carefully selected by the shop's owner, Sumiko Chotikavan. She also designs new silver jewellery and garments inspired by her collection, as well as simple clothes woven in colourful hemp or marihuana fibre. Recommended.
⊞ E11 ✉ Room 301, 3rd floor, River City Shopping Complex, 23 Thanon Yotha, off Thanon Sri Phraya ☎ 237 0077/8 ext 301 🚍 Non-A/C bus 36, 93 ⛴ Sri Phraya pier

THE HEIGHT

Beautiful shop with a vast collection of miniature wooden boats (made to order), 19th-century costumes and silks, and other textiles from all over Southeast Asia, collected by the very knowledgeable Ms Wallee Padungsinseth.
⊞ E11 ✉ Rooms 354 and 452–4, River City Shopping Complex, 23 Thanon Yotha, off Thanon Sri Phraya ☎ 237 0077/8 ext 354/452/554 🚍 Non-A/C bus 36, 93 ⛴ Sri Phraya pier

MONOGRAM

One of Bangkok's longest-established antique dealers, with an exquisite collection of top-quality sculpture, woodcarvings and tapestries, and prices to match.
⊞ E11 ✉ Oriental Hotel and Arcade, 48 Soi Oriental ☎ 236 0400 ext 3371 🚍 A/C bus 15 ⛴ Oriental pier

PENG SENG

The place to head when looking for serious antiques – anything from the tiniest miniature porcelain pieces to larger-than-life stone sculptures from temples. The shop covers two floors and will arrange the necessary papers for export.
⊞ G10 ✉ 942/1–3 Thanon Rama IV, corner of Thanon Surawong ☎ 236 8010 🚍 A/C bus 2, 7

PIECE OF ART

Tiny shop with a great collection of silks, woodcarvings, porcelain and baskets from all over Southeast Asia.
⊞ E11 ✉ Room 451, River City Shopping Complex, 23 Thanon Yotha, off Thanon Sri Phraya ☎ 237 0077 🚍 Non-A/C bus 36, 93 ⛴ Sri Phraya pier

GEMS & JEWELLERY

BUALAAD

Contemporary jewellery inspired by traditional designs, plus a wonderful collection of stones. Stands apart from most other jewellery stores in Bangkok.

🕂 H9 ✉ 106–7 Peninsula Plaza, 153 Thanon Ratchadamri ☎ 253 9790 🚌 A/C bus 4, 5, 15

FRANK'S JEWELRY CREATION

Very ritzy jeweller to both Thai and international stars, with some of the most extravagant and ornate jewels in town. Prices are equally sky-high, but Frank will replicate any piece of jewellery.

🕂 H9 ✉ Shop no 104, Peninsula Plaza, 153 Thanon Ratchadamri ☎ 254 4528 🕐 Mon–Sat 10–6 🚌 A/C bus 4, 5, 15

JOHNNY'S GEMS

One of the city's oldest jewellery emporiums, with a selection to suit all budgets.

🕂 D9 ✉ 199 Thanon Fueng Nakorn, Chinatown ☎ 222 1706 🚌 Telephone for a free shuttle between the shop and your hotel

LOTUS ARTS DE VIVRE

Elegant and stylish shops with exquisite new and old jewellery and *objets d'art* from all over Asia. Suitably expensive.

✉ Branches at the Regent and Sukhothai hotels (➤ 84), and at the Oriental (➤ 39)

ORIENTAL GOLD CIE

An excellent place to find simple gold jewellery at reasonable prices, most often priced by weight.

🕂 G11 ✉ 116/1 Thanon Silom ☎ 238 2715 🕐 Mon–Fri 10:30–7; Sat 11–6 🚌 A/C bus 2, 4, 5, 15

PENINSULA GEMS

Very fine, top-quality jewellery. The selection of diamond rings and bracelets is particularly good.

🕂 H9 ✉ Regent Hotel, 155 Thanon Ratchadamri ☎ 250 0720 🚌 A/C bus 4, 5, 15

TOK KWANG

Famous for selling Bangkok's best pearls, in all price ranges, as well as a large selection of other jewels and gems.

🕂 F11 ✉ 224/226 Thanon Silom ☎ 233 0658 🚌 A/C bus 2, 4, 5, 15

UTHAI'S GEMS

Very reliable jeweller with more conservative designs at good prices, known for its excellent custom work. Also does mail order.

🕂 J9 ✉ 28/7 Soi Ruam Ruedi, off Thanon Ploenchit ☎ 253 8582 🚌 A/C bus 1, 8

YVES JOAILLIER

Yves Bernardeau is the 'darling' of Bangkok's Thai upper-class and expat women. His beautiful and (all things considered) reasonably priced designs are often inspired by ancient jewels from the Mediterranean region. He will also undertake commissions. Strongly recommended.

🕂 H11 ✉ 3rd floor, Charn Issara Tower, Thanon Rama IV ☎ 233 3292 🚌 A/C bus 7

Beware of touts!

Touts hang around all of Bangkok's main shopping areas, and for the unsuspecting shopper they mean trouble. Shop around before buying and remember that it is quite acceptable to bargain, even in more up-market stores. For an insight into the gem market, read John Hoskin's entertaining *Buyer's Guide to Thai Gems* (Asia Books, Bangkok 1988). Locals are often happiest to recommend jewellers in hotel shopping arcades for their reliability.

SILK & FABRICS

Thai silk

The tradition of silk-making goes back hundreds of years in Thailand, but by the early 20th century Thais preferred cheaper imported fabrics and the industry went into decline. Old skills were being lost when Jim Thompson (➤ 41) discovered a few silk-weavers near his house, which gave him the idea of reviving the business. Jim Thompson's Thai Silk Company Ltd was founded in 1948 and was well reviewed in *Vogue*. Two years later he was commissioned to make the costumes for the Broadway production of *The King and I* and his success was assured. He is now referred to as the 'King of Thai Silk'.

ANITA THAI SILK

Often recommended by expats as the place to find reasonably priced and good-quality silk. Wide selection of fabrics, plus men's shirts and ties.

✚ F11 ✉ 294/4–5 Thanon Silom ☎ 234 2481 ⓘ Mon–Sat 8–6 🚌 A/C bus 2, 4, 5, 15

DESIGN THAI

Three floors of silk fabrics, clothes and accessories, with furnishing fabrics, silk place-mats, toys and brightly coloured silk-rag carpets in the basement of the shop.

✚ F11 ✉ 304 Thanon Silom ☎ 235 1553 🚌 A/C bus 2, 4, 5, 15

HOME MADE THAI SILK

Excellent-quality silk, woven on the spot by Thai women working to traditional patterns.

✚ Off map at K10 ✉ 43 Prom Chai Prom Pongse, Sukhumwit Soi 39 ☎ 258 8766 🚌 A/C bus 1, 8, 11, 13

HOMESPUN CREATIONS NANDAKAWANG

The place for home-spun cotton fabrics, tablecloths, place-mats, napkins and cushion covers in wonderful colours and at very reasonable prices. Other branches of this outlet are located on the 5th floor of the Zen Department Store in the World Trade Center, and on the 5th floor of the Emporium Shopping Complex on Sukhumwit Soi 24.

✚ Off map at K10 ✉ 108/3 Sukhumwit Soi 23, Prasanmitr, Klong Doei ☎ 258 1962 🚌 A/C bus 1, 8, 11, 13

JIM THOMPSON'S THAI SILK COMPANY

Not the cheapest place to buy silks or silk clothing, but the quality and the wide variety of colours and textures is superior to most other places, and the name is international currency (see panel). Don't miss the excellent furnishing fabrics, both cotton and silk.

✚ G10/11 ✉ 9 Thanon Surawong ☎ 234 4900 🚌 A/C bus 2, 7

PHA THAI

A great place for cotton and silk fabrics in contemporary designs and good colours.

✚ Off map at K10 ✉ 1/6 Sukhumwit Soi 39 ☎ 259 6617 🚌 A/C bus 1, 8, 11, 13,

PHAHURAT MARKET

(➤ 52)

PRAYER TEXTILE GALLERY

Lovely collection of both old and new traditional textiles from northern Thailand, Laos and Cambodia, as well as some ready-made garments.

✚ G9 ✉ Corner of Siam Square and Thanon Phaya Thai ☎ 251 7549 ⓘ Mon–Sat 10–6 🚌 A/C bus 1, 2, 8, 29

T SHINAWATRA THAI SILK

Wide range of basic cottons and silks, all very reasonably priced. Next door is the factory where some of the fabrics are woven.

✚ Off map at K10 ✉ 94 Sukhumwit Soi 23 ☎ 258 0295 🚌 A/C bus 1, 8, 11, 13

MEN'S CLOTHING

AMBASSADOR INTERNATIONAL CLOTHING

Experienced tailors who have won several awards. They offer quick, cheap packages, but give them adequate time if you want something more refined. Free pick-up service.

🚹 J9 ✉ 1/10–11 Soi Chaiyayot, Sukhumwit Soi 11 (opposite the side entrance of the Ambassador Hotel) ☎ 651 0302/5 🕐 Mon–Sat 10–8 🚌 A/C bus 1, 8, 11, 13

ART'S TAILOR

A proper tailor's shop with a very good reputation. Unlike some other tailors in the city, Art's needs two to three weeks and several fittings to make a suit, but regulars insist that it's worth the wait.

🚹 G11 ✉ 62/15–16 Thanon Thaniya, off Thanon Silom ☎ 236 7966 🚌 A/C bus 2, 4, 5, 15

BAUMAN TAILORS

This excellent shop, recommended by many loyal customers, will make shirts and suits to measure in 24–48 hours. It also has a fine selection of fabrics.

🚹 E11 ✉ Room 207–8, 2nd floor, River City Shopping Complex, 23 Thanon Yotha, off Thanon Sri Phraya ☎ 237 0077/8 ext 208 🚌 Non-A/C bus 36, 93 ⛴ Sri Phraya pier

CHOISY

French-owned and managed tailor, popular with expats, offering top-quality tailored clothes and stylish ready-made garments. Renowned for superior fabrics.

🚹 G11 ✉ 9/25 Thanon Surawong ☎ 233 7794

🕐 Mon–Sat 10–6:30 🚌 A/C bus 2, 7

JIM THOMPSON'S THAI SILK COMPANY

Top-quality, top-priced silk shirts and ties, in a wide though conservative range of patterns and colours, as well as jackets, pyjamas and robes. Other branches are located in Isetan, World Trade Center, and Emporium Shopping Complex.

🚹 G10/11 ✉ 9 Thanon Surawong ☎ 234 4900 🚌 A/C bus 2, 7

NARRY'S BOUTIQUE

Voted 'Tailor of the Year' for several years running. Good-quality work and very quick service. Phone to arrange a free pick-up.

🚹 J9 ✉ 155/22 Thanon Sukhumwit Soi 11/1, near Ambassador Hotel ☎ 651 0180/2 🚌 A/C bus 1, 8, 11, 13

RAJA'S

Renowned tailor, favoured by the diplomatic community in this area, with a good selection of high-quality fabrics.

🚹 J9 ✉ 1/6 Sukhumwit Soi 4, opposite Nana Hotel ☎ 253 8379 🚌 A/C bus 1, 8, 11, 13

TONY'S FASHION HOUSE

Well-established tailors, often recommended by the five-star hotels as the best for both men and women. Has a large variety of both winter and summer fabrics, and the tailors do a good job. Phone for a free pick-up.

🚹 H7 ✉ 90/6–7 Thanon Ratchaphrarop ☎ 246 4703 🚌 A/C bus 4, 15, 13

Tailor-made clothes

Bangkok tailors, mostly Thais of Indian origin, are slowly but surely taking over from their Hong Kong brothers. Good tailors can be found in all tourist areas and in the major hotel shopping arcades. Again, it pays to shop around and to bargain as there is no such thing as a fixed price. Choose good-quality fabric, allow more than the promised 24 hours if you can, and don't expect something for nothing.

WOMEN'S CLOTHING

Shopping-centre boom

The last few years have seen many smaller and a few huge shopping centres rise up above Bangkok's skyline. The best places to look for women's fashion, in particular the more expensive labels, are around Thanon Ploenchit and Thanon Sukhumwit. Amarin Plaza, on Thanon Ploenchit, houses the Sogo department store as well as many other boutiques. Peninsula Plaza, on Thanon Ratchadamri, has a more exclusive selection of shops, including the biggest Versace store in Asia. The largest of all, the World Trade Center on Rajprasongi, has just about everything.

CHARN ISSARA TOWER

This up-market and ultra-stylish shopping centre has several floors with some of the best women's fashion in town. Don't forget to take a loaded wallet as the temptations are plentiful.

🛨 H11 ✉ 942/86 Thanon Rama IV ⏱ Mon–Sat 10–8 🚌 A/C bus 7

COMMON TRIBE

Minimalist Thai-style clothes and shoes in natural fabrics and neutral colours (mostly black and white), plus distinctive jewellery made from fish and camel bone, glass, resin, silver and amber.

🛨 J3 ✉ Section 24, Soi 2, Chatuchak Weekend Market (▶ 46) ☎ 456 2132 ⏱ Sat–Sun 11–6 🚌 A/C bus 2, 3, 10, 13, 29

EMPORIUM SHOPPING COMPLEX

Major international designers such as Gucci, Prada and Paul Smith have all set up shop here recently, as have some local names. This is one of the more exciting shopping centres, with up-market restaurants and several cinemas.

🛨 Off map at K10 ✉ Sukhumwit Soi 24 🚌 A/C bus 1, 8, 11, 13

GAYSORN PLAZA

Exclusive shopping centre with the latest fashions from current international designers such as Prada, Katherine Hamnett and Max Mara.

🛨 H9 ✉ Thanon Gesorn, off Thanon Ploenchit 🚌 A/C bus 1, 4, 5, 8, 11, 13, 15

JASPAL

Simply styled contemporary fashion, mostly in plain colours and at reasonable prices. Other branches of the store are located at the Siam Center (☎ 251 5918) and the Charn Issara Tower (☎ 234 7484).

🛨 H9 ✉ Amarin Plaza Shopping Centre, 500 Thanon Ploenchit ☎ 256 9009 🚌 A/C bus 1, 4, 5, 8, 11, 13, 15

KHANITHA

Glamorous and brightly coloured evening dresses and short suits in less conservative designs.

🛨 E11 ✉ Room 262, River City Shopping Complex, 23 Thanon Yotha, off Thanon Sri Phraya ☎ 237 0077 ext 262 🚌 Non-A/C bus 36, 93 ⛴ Sri Phraya pier

RIVER MARK

One of the best and least conservative tailors for women, specialising in linen suits, but also with a large selection of silk and wool fabrics. Also at 1287–9 Thanon Charoen Krung (New Road).

🛨 E11 ✉ Room 238, 2nd floor, River City Shopping Complex, 23 Thanon Yotha, off Thanon Sri Phraya ☎ 237 0077/8 ext 238 🚌 Non-A/C bus 36, 93 ⛴ Sri Phraya pier

SHA

A small selection of silk and roughly woven cotton clothing and shawls, as well as lovely *mutmee* silks and accessories.

🛨 E11 ✉ Room 316, River City Shopping Complex, 23 Thanon Yotha, off Thanon Sri Phraya ☎ 237 0077 ext 316 🚌 Non-A/C bus 36, 93 ⛴ Sri Phraya pier

CRAFTS

GIFTED HANDS

Cholada Hoover's wonderful shop sells her own jewellery, inspired by traditional designs from the villages and using glass beads, as well as nielloware jewellery.

Off map at K9 ✉ 172/18 Sukhumwit Soi 23 ☎ 258 4010 🚍 A/C bus 1, 8, 11, 13

HILL TRIBE FOUNDATION

This project, supported by the royal family, offers hill-tribe crafts at reasonable prices, all the profits returning to the tribespeople living in the villages of northern Thailand. The Chit Lada Shop is a similar project at the Chit Lada Palace, Thanon Rama V (☎ 281 4558).

G9 ✉ Saprathum Palace 195, Thanon Phraya Thai ☎ 351 9816 🕓 Mon–Fri 9–5 🚍 A/C bus 1, 2, 8, 29

HOUSE OF HANDICRAFTS

An amazing variety of well-made crafts, dolls and textiles from Thailand, Laos and Myanmar (Burma), with plenty of ideas for gifts.

H9 ✉ Courtyard of the Regent Hotel, 155 Thanon Ratchadamri ☎ 250 0724 🚍 A/C bus 4, 5, 15

MOTIF & MARIS

Large selection of cotton and silk fabrics, carved wooden boxes, lacquerware, home accessories, celadon, and lovely cotton animals and nursery toys. Specialises in hand-smocked girls' dresses. Other branches are located at the Silom Village Trade Centre, 286 Thanon Silom (☎ 237 8454) and the Ambassador Hotel, 8 Thanon Sukhumwit (☎ 254 0444 ext 1147).

E11 ✉ Room 220, River City Shopping Complex, 23 Thanon Yotha, off Thanon Sri Phraya ☎ 237 0077/8 ext 220 🚍 Non-A/C bus 36, 93 ⛴ Sri Phraya pier

NARAYANA PHAND PAVILION

A huge crafts and souvenir emporium that sells everything. Usually good value.

H9 ✉ 127 Thanon Ratchadamri, north of Thanon Gesorn ☎ 252 4670 🚍 A/C bus 4, 5, 11, 13, 15

RASI SAYAM

This old wooden house is filled with a wonderful collection of fine Thai handicrafts, pottery, baskets, woodwork and textiles, some old, some very contemporary, but all carefully selected and reasonably priced by enthusiastic manager Jonathan Hayssen. Recommended.

Off map at K9 ✉ 32 Sukhumwit Soi 23 ☎ 258 4195/3575 🚍 A/C bus 1, 8, 11, 13

THAI HOME INDUSTRIES

Dusty teak house full of baskets, cotton farmers' clothes, temple bells, glass lamps and, above all, the company's stylish and now much-copied bronze and metal cutlery. They do mail order and will ship whatever you like.

E11 ✉ 35 Soi Oriental ☎ 234 1736 🚍 A/C bus 2 ⛴ Oriental pier

Thai design

Mrs Shinawatra, who owns T Shinawatra Thai Silk (➤ 72), recently opened Thailand's answer to Habitat. Her bright new shop, Homework (✉ 136 Sukhumwit Soi 23 ☎ 259 1301), has everything you need for the house, all designed and made by Thais.

More art galleries

About Café and About Studio (✉ 402–8 Thanon Maitri Chit, near Hua Lamphong Station ☎ 623 1742/3 🕓 Mon–Fri 7PM–midnight; Sat–Sun 7PM–2AM) is a very happening place showing modern art, but also stages music, Chinese opera, Thai culinary art shows and the like. 303 Open Space (✉ 3rd floor, 303 Coop Housing Building, 1129/63 Thanon Turi Damri ☎ 668 4651 🕓 Wed–Sun noon–6PM) is a non-commercial forum for young contemporary artists, while Project 304 (✉ 304 Coop Housing Building, 1129/64 Thanon Turi Damri ☎ 668 5151 🕓 Wed–Sun 10AM–6PM, or by appointment) is an avant-garde gallery. For more information ➤ 47.

75

CRAFT FACTORIES

Hand-made baskets

Many general craft shops sell some of Thailand's finest baskets, but there are a few shops that specialise in them. Song Plu, in room 425 of the River City Shopping Complex (➤ 38), has one of the best selections of old and new baskets. A few shops on Thanon Maha Chai, near the intersection with Thanon Luang (🞧 D8/9), sell cheaper and more practical baskets, often made in the nearby prison. There are also baskets on sale at the Chatuchak Weekend Market (➤ 46).

BANGKOK DOLLS

Exquisite hand-made dolls dressed in clothes and jewellery typically worn by hill-tribe people and classical Thai dancers. Well worth the trip.
🞧 Off map ✉ 85 Soi Ratchatapan (Soi Mohleng), Makkasan, about an hour by car from Bangkok ☎ 245 3008
❓ Best reached by taxi

BLUE AND WHITE POTTERIES

Small family-run business producing excellent-quality pottery and selling it cheaper than elsewhere.
🞧 Off map at B1 ✉ Surachai Nuparwan, Oum Noi, Samut Sakhon, on the way to the Rose Garden Country Resort (➤ 81 panel) 🚌 Regular buses from Bangkok's Southern Bus Terminal to Nakhom Pathom, but easier by taxi

BUDDHA CASTING

After spending a few days strolling around various temple compounds, you may be interested to see one of the places where Buddha images are cast.
🞧 A8 ✉ Just off Thanon Phrannok, next door to Wat Wiset Khan 🕐 Mon–Sat (just pass by to see if they are working) 🚢 Cross-river ferry from Phra Chan pier to Phrannok pier

GOLD LEAF FACTORY

Interesting crafts factory where you can watch gold being beaten into thin gold leaf. The shop is opposite Wat Bowon Niwet at 321 Thanon Phra Sumen.
🞧 C8 ✉ Off Thanon Ratchadamnoen Klang, behind post office and near Democracy Monument 🚌 A/C bus 3, 6, 9, 11, 12, 39, 44

MONKS' BOWLS

Of the three original villages, just one street remains where artisans make the black-lacquer monks' bowls from steel, wood and copper. Only a few families still produce them, and not every day, but you can always buy them from these houses. More monks' bowls and robes are on sale on Thanon Bamrung Muang near Wat Suthat and the Giant Swing (➤ 51).
🞧 D8 ✉ Soi Bahn Bat, off Thanon Worachak 🚌 A/C bus 8

SIAM BRONZE FACTORIES

Get a glimpse of the Thai bronze-working tradition, apparently the oldest in the world, and see some of the country's most beautiful cutlery being made. The finished products are also on sale in the showroom.
🞧 E11/12 ✉ 1250 Thanon Charoen Krung (New Road) ☎ 234 9436 🕐 Call for an appointment 🚌 A/C bus 2, 4, 5, 15

SN BRONZE FACTORY

Showroom and factory of beautiful bronze cutlery and plates. Very good prices.
🞧 H8 ✉ Soi Samran, 157/33 Thanon Phetburi ☎ 215 8941 🚌 A/C bus 4, 5, 11, 12, 13

THAI SILK-WEAVING

It is possible to see silk-weaving at the T Shinawatra factory and at Home Made Thai Silk (➤ 72).

BEST OF THE REST

ASIA BOOKS

Offers the best selection of English-language books in the city, with a large choice of titles on Bangkok, Thailand, Thai culture and other Asian countries. Other branches are located at 221 Thanon Sukhumvit, Landmark Plaza and Thaniya Plaza, near Thanon Silom.

➕ H9 ✉ 2nd floor, Peninsula Plaza, 153 Thanon Ratchadamri ☎ 253 9786 🚌 A/C bus 4, 5, 15

CHAI LAI

Excellent silver jewellery from the hill tribes, plus attractive old Thai jewellery. Pure ethnic chic.

➕ H9 ✉ 1st floor, Peninsula Plaza, 153 Thanon Ratchadamri ☎ 252 1538 🚌 A/C bus 4, 5, 15

ELITE USED BOOKS

Foreign-language books tend to be expensive in Thailand, so Elite offers good-value second-hand books, mainly in English, but also in German, Japanese, French and Dutch. They also buy or trade in used books in good condition, but their rates are usually pretty low.

➕ Off map at K10 ✉ 593/5 Thanon Sukhumvit, near Soi 33 ☎ 258 0221 🕙 Daily 9–9 🚌 A/C bus 1, 8, 11, 13

KINOKUNIYA

Thailand's largest English bookshop, with a wide range of both locally printed and imported books. Another branch is located in the Emporium Shopping Complex (➤ 74).

➕ H9 ✉ 6th Floor, Isetan, World Trade Center, Thanon Ratchadamri ☎ 255 9834/6 🚌 A/C bus 4, 11, 13, 15

MANILA FURNITURE

Good-quality rattan and wicker furniture, ready-made or to your own design, can be shipped back home. Also check out the similar Italy Furniture next door.

➕ Off map at K10 ✉ 521 Thanon Sukhumvit, near Soi 29 ☎ 258 2608 🚌 A/C bus 1, 8, 11, 13

PADUNG CHIIP

This large but crowded shop sells the intricate papier-mâché masks worn by classical Thai dancers, as well as masks of animals and colourful mobiles made from banana leaves.

➕ C7 ✉ Corner of Thanon Drok Mayom and Thanon Chakkaphong, just south of Thanon Khao San ☎ 281 6664 🚌 A/C bus 3, 6, 9, 11, 12, 39, 44

SPIRIT HOUSES

Several open-air shops selling spirit houses (➤ 32, panel) and accessories in all sizes and colours.

➕ J8 ✉ Thanon Phetburi, just past the expressway bridge 🚌 A/C bus 12

THAI CELADON HOUSE

This showroom for the Chiang Mai factory has some of the finest celadon ceramics in town and offers excellent value.

➕ K10 ✉ 8/6–8 Sukhumvit Soi 16 (Soi Asoke) ☎ 259 7744 🚌 A/C bus 1, 8, 11, 13

Business cards and stationery

It is no problem if you run out of much-needed business cards in Bangkok as it is a cheap place to have them printed. There are laser-printing booths in most major department stores and shopping centres, but for something more exotic head for the 'Printers Street', or Thanon Phat Sai (➕ E10), off Thanon Song Sawat (where other than in Chinatown?). Bangkok residents also go to the Assumption Cathedral near the Oriental Hotel for printing and bookbinding.

BARS

One night in Bangkok

Bangkok has the liveliest nightlife in Asia, with much more to it than the sex clubs in Patpong and on Soi Cowboy. Many bars have live music, usually jazz, pop or Thai pop, and provide food as well. Thais believe life should be *sanuk*, or fun, something that becomes very clear once offices and shops have shut, and workers head off for a good meal before going on to a bar.

ABSTRACT FUN PUB

Part of the lively bar scene at Chatuchak Weekend Market. This venue in particular is filled with angry young Thais bouncing to very loud live bands that play covers of Nirvana and Radiohead.
➕ J3 ✉ Sunday Plaza Soi 3, Chatuchak Weekend Market (➤ 46) 🕐 Sat–Sun noon–10PM 🚌 A/C bus 2, 3, 10, 13, 29

BAMBOO BAR

A tastefully decorated and cosy bar with a barman who knows how to handle his shaker. After 10PM there are live jazz bands, often from the USA.
➕ E11 ✉ Oriental Hotel, 48 Soi Oriental ☎ 236 0400 ext 3108 🕐 Sun–Thu 11AM–1AM; Fri–Sat 11AM–2AM 🚌 A/C bus 4, 15 ⛴ Oriental pier

BLUE NOTE

Popular bar with a laid-back atmosphere. The music is as varied as the customers, who come here to unwind over a few beers and the tasty Thai snacks.
➕ Off map at K10 ✉ 6/10–11 Sukhumvit Soi 22 ☎ 260 3921 🕐 Mon–Sat 5PM–1am (6–9PM is happy hour) 🚌 A/C bus 1, 8, 11, 13

BLUES BAR

Pathumwan's trendiest bar is popular with well-heeled and arty young Thais. Good music, very laid-back atmosphere and the beer is cheap. Good Thai food.
➕ H10 ✉ 231/16 Soi Sarasin, off Thanon Ratchadamri ☎ 252 7335 🕐 Mon–Fri 6PM–1AM; Sat–Sun 6PM–midnight 🚌 A/C bus 4, 5

BOBBY'S ARMS

The closest you'll get in Bangkok to an English pub, and very popular with Anglophiles and older expats. Bobby's serves traditional British cuisine for lunch and dinner, and has live music on Friday, Saturday and Sunday evenings.
➕ G11 ✉ 114/1–2 Thanon Silom, Thanon Patpong 2, 1st floor of car park ☎ 233 6828 🕐 Daily 11AM–1AM 🚌 A/C bus 2, 4, 5, 15

BOH

Open in the late afternoon, but particularly lively in the evening, this café-on-the-pier is very popular with students. The latest Thai rock music and cheap beer, plus a fantastic river view.
➕ B9 ✉ Tian pier, Thanon Maha Rat 🕐 Daily 7PM–midnight ⛴ Tian pier

BROWN SUGAR

Wildly popular and therefore often very crowded, with some of Bangkok's best live music every night (country, jazz or blues). On Tuesdays there is a performance by Thailand's best jazz musician, Tewan Sapsenyakorn. Reasonably priced menu with both Thai and European food.
➕ H10 ✉ 231/20 Soi Sarasin, opposite Lumphini Park ☎ 250 0103 🕐 Mon–Sat 11AM–1AM; Sun 5PM–1AM 🚌 A/C bus 4, 5, 15

HARD ROCK CAFÉ

Another one! Friendly family burger restaurant in the Hard Rock Café tradition, with yet another rock 'n' roll museum.

T-shirts are cheaper in the night markets.

🏠 G9 ✉ 424/3–6 Soi Siam Square 11 ☎ 251 0792/4 🕐 Daily 11AM–2AM 🚌 A/C bus 1, 2, 8, 18, 29

KHLUENZAK, FM 108.5 PUB

Popular bar-restaurant frequented mainly by young, well-dressed Thais. The sign is only in Thai, so look out for the FM 108.5 bit underneath.

🏠 Off map at K10 ✉ 1/8 Sukhumwit Soi 24 ☎ 258 6822 🕐 Daily 5:30PM–1AM 🚌 A/C bus 1, 8, 11, 13

KOOL SPOT

Dance-music bar with a mosaic-tiled counter in the shape of a snake.

🏠 G11 ✉ 114/6 Silom Soi 4 ☎ 266 4820 🕐 Mon–Thu, Sun 9PM–3AM; Fri–Sat 9PM–5AM 🚌 A/C bus 2, 4, 5, 15

PARADISE BAR

Thanon Khao San is the bar area of the moment, and this place is one of the most popular hang-outs for young Thais, travellers and laid-back expats alike.

🏠 C7 ✉ Down alley through tape shop (opposite Chart Guest House), Thanon Khao San 🕐 Daily 6PM–very late 🚌 A/C bus 3, 6, 9, 12, 39, 44

SAXOPHONE

One of Bangkok's few very late-night haunts, long established with live jazz, rock or reggae and a clientele always in the party mood. Also Thai and European food.

🏠 G7 ✉ 3/8 Victory Monument, Thanon Phaya Thai ☎ 246 5472 🕐 5PM–5AM 🚌 A/C bus 2, 3, 9, 10, 13, 14, 29, 39

STUDIO WEST

This is the place to go if you want the party to last and last. Upstairs has good dance music, while downstairs is slightly quieter.

🏠 H7 ✉ 90/30–1 Thanon Ratchaprarop ☎ 245 7417 🕐 Daily 8PM–6AM or later 🚌 A/C bus 4, 13, 15

TAWANNA

This is the place to hear live contemporary Thai music, as the Tawanna always tries to feature the most promising young talents in town. Good Thai food, too.

🏠 G11 ✉ Tawanna Ramada Hotel, 80 Thanon Surawong ☎ 236 0361 🕐 Closes 1AM 🚌 A/C bus 2, 7

TIARA BAR

The Tiara, located at the top of the Dusit Thani Hotel, is one of the city's famous rooms with a view. It is perfect for a quiet afternoon tea, for watching the sunset or for a romantic aperitif before dining in one of the hotel's superb restaurants.

🏠 G11 ✉ Dusit Thani Hotel, Thanon Rama IV, near Thanon Silom ☎ 236 0450 🕐 11AM–midnight 🚌 A/C bus 2, 4, 5, 7, 15

THE WALL

Popular bar-cum-restaurant, especially lively late at night. Drinks are quite cheap and the menu offers a strange mixture of North European and New Zealand specialities. Situated in the backwaters of Thanon Silom.

🏠 F11 ✉ Soi Pramot 3, off Soi Mahesak 🕐 Daily 2PM–1AM 🚌 A/C bus 2, 4, 5, 15

Gay bars

If you are interested in sampling Bangkok's very active gay scene, start off at the bars around Rome Club (➤ 80) on Soi Patpong 4, or those on Soi Patpong 2 off Thanon Silom. Another gay hang-out is the area around Sukhumwit Soi 23. Here you will find Utopia (✉ 116/1 Sukhumwit Soi 23, opposite Tia Maria ☎ 259 9619), Southeast Asia's first gay/lesbian community venue, offering a shop and café. Pick up the free gay magazine, *Pink Ink*, for listings of gay venues.

Cigar lounges

Bangkok has not escaped the craze for posing with and enjoying cigars, and there are now several cigar lounges. The Oriental Hotel has a Davidoff shop, while the Regent's lobby is a great place to sample over 60 malt whiskies and 30 imported cigars. The Private Cellar (✉ Pavillion Y, RCA New Thanon Phetburi ☎ 203 0926) and a new wine bar called Sip'N'Puff – A Perfect Evening (✉ Ruam Ruedi Village, Soi Ruam Ruedi, off Thanon Ploenchit) are both perfect places to turn up with a huge Havana.

CLUBS & DISCOS

Admission charges

Many discothèques will charge a hefty cover charge, which usually includes one or two drinks. These charges are often doubled on Friday and Saturday evenings, but that's when the fun is to be had (discos tend to be quite dull during weekdays). Beware that innocent foreigners are sometimes overcharged.

A Thai night out

For a typical Thai evening out with nightly performances of Thai pop by local singers and bands, try the Nile Club ✉ Mandarin Bangkok Hotel, 662 Thanon Rama IV ☎ 238 0230 ⏰ Daily 7–1 🎟 Admission charge.

CONCEPT CM2

This multi-theme club has several entertainment areas, including the red zone Club de la Femme, which is for women only. There is live music every evening starting at 9:30 and 11:30.
➕ G9 ✉ Novotel, Siam Square Soi 6 ☎ 255 6888 ⏰ Daily 7PM–2AM 🚌 A/C bus 1, 8, 11, 13 🎟 Admission charge

THE PEPPERMINT

Popular bar where every-one – from tourist couples, resident expats and Thai girls – gathers after other bars have closed. Dancing to good music.
➕ G11 ✉ Thanon Patpong 1, off Thanon Silom ⏰ No fixed hours, best after 1AM 🚌 A/C bus 2, 4, 5, 15

NARCISSUS

An excellent disco, recently redecorated in baroque style. It offers a good mixture of hip-hop, rock, house and techno, plus anything else the DJ feels like playing.
➕ Off map at K10 ✉ 112 Sukhumwit Soi 23 (first turning on the right) ☎ 258 2549 ⏰ Daily 9PM–2AM 🚌 A/C bus 1, 8, 11, 13 🎟 Admission charge

ROME CLUB

This is a great place for a night out on the town, with a trendy and very mixed clientele. It has good music and stages a very camp transvestite show.
➕ G11 ✉ 90–6 Soi Patpong 4, off Thanon Silom ☎ 233 8836 ⏰ Every night, good after midnight 🚌 A/C bus 2, 4, 5, 15 🎟 Admission charge

SPASSO

The hippest Italian restaurant in town, full of bright young things, which dishes out delicious Italian pastas and thin-crust pizzas. At 10:30PM a live band kicks into action and the place turns into a trendy club.
➕ H9 ✉ Grand Hyatt Erawan, 494 Thanon Ratchadamri ☎ 254 1234 ⏰ Lunch, dinner (until late) 🚌 A/C bus 1, 4, 5, 8, 15

TAURUS

Very chic and up-market nightclub complex on several levels, frequented by well-dressed Thais and *farangs*. Check out the *sushi* bar, pub or restaurant first, but make sure you end up in the large balconied disco with its excellent dance music.
➕ Off map at K10 ✉ Sukhumwit Soi 26, beside Four Wings Hotel ☎ 261 3991 ⏰ Daily 6:30PM–2AM 🚌 A/C bus 1, 8, 11, 13

T-BAR

Formerly known as Deeper, this popular disco still plays the best rave music in town even though the atmosphere is now slightly more restrained.
➕ G11 ✉ 82 Silom Soi 4 ☎ 233 2830 ⏰ Daily 10PM–2AM 🚌 A/C bus 2, 4, 5, 15

THAI DANCE

Once only seen at the royal court, elegant classical Thai dance and drama is now performed as entertainment for Thai people and tourists alike.

The most sophisticated form of dance, known as *khon*, invariably represents the war between Rama, the righteous king and a reincarnation of the Hindu god Vishnu, and Thotsakan, the king of the demons. At the heart of this drama – full of passion, love and war – is the abduction of Rama's beloved by Thotsakan.

Singing and speaking are performed by reciters and singers, who stand beside the stage, while the players – apart from the clowns, who can speak for themselves – concentrate on acting or dancing their parts. As the steps and poses of the dancers must conform meticulously to the narrative as told by songs and recitations, and by the music of the small orchestra, they require a strict training from childhood. Demons and monkeys wear masks, while humans and celestial beings appear barefaced.

In addition to the venues listed below, some hotels and restaurants offer cultural shows, usually a mixture of *khon*, sword-fighting and folk dances (➤ 64).

CHALERMKRUNG ROYAL THEATRE
Recently restored Thai deco building where excellent and very sophisticated *khon* spectacles are performed. Tickets don't come cheap and it's an occasion to dress up for.
🕂 C9 ✉ Corner of Thanon Charoen Krung (New Road) and Thanon Tripetch ☎ 225 8757/8 🕔 Normally Tue and Thu at 8PM, but schedules may vary 🚌 A/C bus 1, 7, 8,

DANCE CENTRE
Organises performances by both international and Thai dance groups, often in aid of local charities
🕂 Off map at K10 ✉ 53/3 Sukhumwit Soi 33 ☎ 251 9638 🚌 A/C bus 1, 8, 11, 13

ERAWAN SHRINE
(➤ 44)

LAK MUANG
(➤ 32)

NATIONAL THEATRE
Performances of classical dance and music by students of the School of Music and Dance are often excellent.
🕂 B7 ✉ 1 Thanon Naphratad, near the National Museum ☎ 221 4885 🕔 Check with Thai Tourist Authority (☎ 226 0060) or the box office 🚌 A/C bus 3, 6, 7, 9, 11, 39

THAILAND CULTURAL CENTRE
Modern theatre, venue for concerts by the Bangkok Symphony Orchestra, as well as drama and classical Thai dance.
🕂 Off map at K5/6 ✉ Thanon Ratchadaphisek, Huai Khwang ☎ 247 0028 🕔 Check for performance dates 🚌 A/C bus 15, 18, 22

Tourist-oriented performances
The Rose Garden Country Resort, a popular but very touristy day-trip from Bangkok, offers a Thai cultural show with mainly *khon* and folk dances, and an explanation about Thai culture
🕂 Off map at A11 ✉ On Highway 4 to Nakhom Pathom ☎ 225 3261 🕔 Daily 8–6, show at 3 🚌 Buses leave from Bangkok's Southern Bus Terminal.

CINEMA & THEATRE

The King and I

Despite its popularity elsewhere, the film *The King and I* was not appreciated in Thailand and is still banned. The film was based on the memoirs of Anna Leonowens, an Englishwoman brought to Thailand in the 19th century by King Rama IV to educate his children (➤ 12). Thais insist that Ms Leonowens' memoirs were fiction, not fact, and however splendid some may find Yul Brynner, locals are insulted by his portrayal of their king.

CINEMA

Bangkok's cinemas, most of which are located in shopping centres around Thanon Ploenchit and Thanon Sukhumvit, show Thai, Indian, Chinese and American movies. Films are listed in the *Nation* and *Bangkok Post* daily papers, and in the monthly *Metro* magazine. All movies are preceded by the Thai national anthem, during which images of King Bhumibol and his family are projected.

Thai films are often comedies, or karate or violent movies, all interlaced with intrigue and drama. Many cinemas now show movies with English soundtracks or subtitles. Showing times tend to be the same: daily 2PM, 5PM, 7PM and 9PM, plus 10AM on Saturdays and Sundays. Foreign films may be heavily censored, edited if too long or with the addition of a happy Thai-style ending to please the audience. To see original uncut versions of films, head for one of the cultural centres listed below.

CULTURAL CENTRES AND THEATRES

ALLIANCE FRANÇAISE

The Alliance is very active in Bangkok, offering a busy programme of French films, concerts and lectures.
➕ H11 ✉ 29 Thanon Satorn Tai ☎ 213 2122 🕓 Telephone for programme 🚌 A/C bus 5

BRITISH COUNCIL

The most active of the cultural centres, with regular lectures, films, concerts, music and dance performances.
➕ G9 ✉ 428 Soi Siam Square 2, off Thanon Rama I ☎ 252 6136 🕓 Telephone for programme or check with the English-language newspapers 🚌 A/C bus 1, 2, 8

GOETHE INSTITUT

Limited programme of films, lectures and concerts.
➕ H11 ✉ 18/1 Soi Atthakanprasit, off Thanon Satorn Tai ☎ 287 2822 🕓 Telephone for programme 🚌 A/C bus 5

ORIENTAL HOTEL

The Oriental regularly invites internationally renowned artists, musicians and theatre groups to perform at the hotel. Tickets should usually be booked in advance (➤ 39).

PATRAVADI THEATRE

This outdoor theatre is renowned for its lavish productions, often modern adaptations of classical Asian works, and is popular with an avant-garde audience.
➕ B8 ✉ Soi Wat Ra Kang ☎ 412 7287 🚌 Chang Wang Luang pier, then cross-river ferry to Wat Ra Kang

THAILAND CULTURAL CENTRE

Apart from classical dance performances, the centre regularly hosts international cultural events, art exhibitions and concerts (➤ 81).

SPORTS

HORSE-RACING

ROYAL BANGKOK SPORTS CLUB
➕ G9/10 ✉ Thanon Henri Dunant ☎ 251 0181 🕐 Every other Sun at 12:10PM 🚌 A/C bus 1, 4, 5, 8, 15

ROYAL TURF CLUB
➕ E7 ✉ Thanon Phitsanulok, south of Chit Lada Park ☎ 280 0020/5 🕐 Every other Sun at 12:10PM 🚌 A/C bus 3, 5, 9 💵 Admission fee; betting starts at 50B

KITE FIGHTING

On Sanam Luang (➤ 32).

KRABI-KRABONG (SWORD FIGHTING)

This traditional martial art uses hand-held weapons – in particular the Thai battle sword, or *krabi-krabong*. The modern version, used during matches, blends weapon fighting and Thai boxing. Players are arranged in pairs and often fight with different weapons. For more information on training courses, contact Ajaan Samai Mesamarna at the Buddhai Sawan Fencing School of Thailand (✉ 5/1 Thanon Phetkasem, Thonburi).

T'AI CHI

In Lumphini Park (➤ 45).

TAKRAW

A local variation on volley-ball, where a woven rattan ball is hit between two teams separated by a volleyball net. Only the head and feet can be used (hands are out), which has created a fast and spectacular game. Matches are held throughout the city. For up-to-date information, check with your hotel or call ☎ 465 5325 for dates and times of matches.

NATIONAL STADIUM
The venue for the most important *takraw* matches.
➕ F10 ✉ Thanon Rama I ☎ 214 0121 🕐 Check locally for dates 🚌 A/C bus 8

THAI BOXING (MUAY THAY)

An excessive number of injuries and deaths led to a ban on this sport in the 1920s, but it has returned after popular demand in a stricter form, with contestants now wearing proper gloves and trunks. The sport is, however, still violent as anything seems to go: punching, kicking with the legs, elbow thrusts and even taking an opponent's head between the legs and kicking it with the knee. In spite of the bloodshed, the sport remains extremely popular in Thailand.

LUMPHINI STADIUM
➕ H11 ✉ Thanon Rama IV, near Lumphini Park ☎ 251 4303 🕐 Tue, Fri, Sat from 6:30PM until late 🚌 A/C bus 7

RATCHADAMNOEN STADIUM
➕ D7 ✉ Thanon Ratchadamnoen Nok, near TAT office ☎ 381 0056 🕐 Mon, Wed, Thu from 6PM; Sun from 5PM 🚌 A/C bus 3, 9

Thai boxing training

Thai boxing has become increasingly popular in the West, and as a result many foreigners come to Bangkok to train. The Australian Patrick Cusick organises Thai boxing camps for foreigners at Thai Championship Boxing (✉ PO Box 1996, Bangkok ☎ 234 5360; fax 236 7242). The Pramote Gym (✉ 210–2 Soi Kingphet, Thanon Phetburi, Ratchathewi ☎ 215 1206) also organises training for both locals and foreigners. For a more serious, and often violent, traditional camp try PB Boxing Gym (✉ Thanon Khao San, behind the PB Guesthouse).

LUXURY HOTELS

Prices

Approximate prices for a double room:

Budget	under 1,400B
Mid-range	under 3,800B
Luxury	over 3,800B

Asian luxury

There is no shortage of luxury hotels in Bangkok, and the standards of their rooms and service are amongst the best in the world. Travel agents in Bangkok or your home country often offer substantial discounts on room rates; check that the cost includes breakfast (American buffet or Continental) as it is usually expensive. In the low season most hotels will also reduce their rates by 25–50 per cent when asked.

DUSIT THANI

The Dusit Thani, meaning 'Town in Heaven', certainly lives up to its name, and is an oasis with cascades and fountains in the heart of a very busy area of the city. Its elegant rooms are decorated with Thai silks and teak wood, and many of them overlook the green spaces of Lumphini Park.
✚ G11 ✉ Thanon Rama IV, near Thanon Silom ☎ 236 0450; fax 236 6400 🚌 A/C bus 2, 4, 5, 7, 15

MARRIOTT ROYAL GARDEN RIVERSIDE

A resort hotel on the west bank of the Chao Phraya, with good restaurants (► 67), a tranquil garden and a superb swimming pool. Ideal for those with kids.
✚ Just off map at C13 ✉ 257/1–3 Thanon Charoen Nakorn, near Krung Thep Bridge ☎ 476 0021; fax 476 1120 🚤 Free shuttle boat from Oriental Hotel or River City Shopping Complex pier

ORIENTAL HOTEL

The Oriental is a Bangkok institution (► 39).

REGENT HOTEL

An impressive modern hotel with a grand, old-style atmosphere, an imposing lobby, an excellent shopping arcade and sumptuous, elegant rooms, some overlooking the excellent pool of the Royal Bangkok Sports Club. It is now part of the Four Seasons chain, and boasts near-perfect service.
✚ H9 ✉ 155 Thanon Ratchadamri ☎ 251 6127; fax 253 9195 🚌 A/C bus 4, 5, 15

ROYAL ORCHID SHERATON HOTEL & TOWERS

Luxurious rooms overlooking the Chao Phraya river, a wide choice of restaurants, two riverside swimming pools and use of the pool at the Portuguese Embassy. Convenient location next to the River City Shopping Complex and near the business district.
✚ E11 ✉ 2 Soi Captain Bush, Thanon Sri Phraya ☎ 234 5599; fax 236 8320 🚌 A/C bus 15 🚤 Sri Phraya pier

SHANGRI-LA

An elegant five-star hotel located next door to the Oriental (see above), with most rooms overlooking Thonburi and the river. It has two superb swimming pools set in fragrant gardens with ponds, shrines and a spirit house. The more recent Krungthep Wing offers more luxurious and larger rooms with balconies.
✚ E11 ✉ 89 Soi Wat Suan Plu, off Thanon Charoen Krung ☎ 236 7777; fax 236 8579 🚌 A/C bus 2 🚤 Shangri-La pier

SUKHOTHAI HOTEL

This is a remarkable hotel in the heart of the business district, decorated in a contemporary Thai minimalist style. Spacious guest rooms are decorated with granite, teak and silks. Exceptional service. Equally recommended for its excellent restaurants (► 62 and ► 69, panel).
✚ H11 ✉ 13/3 Thanon Satorn Tai ☎ 287 0222; fax 287 4980 🚌 A/C bus 5

MID-RANGE HOTELS

BOSSOTEL INN

This pleasant and well-located hotel (in a quiet side-street near the river and the big hotels) is very good value. Rooms are clean and spacious, and the lobby has the only kosher restaurant in town.

📍 E11 ✉ 55/8–9 Soi Charoen Krung 42/1, off Thanon Charoen Krung (New Road) ☎ 630 6120; fax 237 3225 🚌 A/C bus 2, 4, 5, 15 🛳 Oriental pier

MAJESTIC PALACE

Bangkok's oldest hotel (built by Rama V) has lost most of its glory, but is still in royal hands and boasts spacious, well-maintained rooms decorated with faded photographs of old Bangkok.

📍 C8 ✉ 97 Thanon Ratchadamnoen Klang, near Democracy Monument ☎ 280 5610; fax 280 0965 🚌 A/C bus 11, 12, 39, 44

MANHATTAN

Modern, good-value hotel in a central location, and with spacious and tastefully decorated rooms. The service is friendly, and there is a good bar and restaurant.

📍 K9 ✉ 13 Sukhumvit Soi 15, near the Ambassador Hotel ☎ 255 0166; fax 255 3481 🚌 A/C bus 1, 8, 11, 13

ROYAL HOTEL

The 1950s-style Royal went through a turbulent patch during the 1991 demonstrations, when it was used as a hospital, but today it is as would-be grand as ever. The slightly aged rooms verge on pure kitsch, but there is a small pool and the Grand Palace and National Museum lie only a short walk away.

📍 C8 ✉ 2 Thanon Ratchadamnoen Klang ☎ 222 9111; fax 224 2083 🚌 A/C bus 3, 6, 9, 11, 12, 44

THE SOMERSET

In the heart of it all, yet tucked down a quiet back lane. Offers comfortable rooms and a 24-hour business centre.

📍 K9 ✉ 10 Sukhumvit Soi 15 ☎ 254 8500; fax 254 8534 🚌 A/C bus 1, 8, 11, 13

TAI-PAN

A modern hotel in a convenient location for restaurants and shopping. The large rooms overlook the city, and there is a swimming pool and business centre. The coffee-shop offers a good buffet lunch.

📍 Off map at K10 ✉ 25 Sukhumvit Soi 23 ☎ 260 9888; fax 259 7908 🚌 A/C bus 1, 8, 11, 13

TOWER INN

Rather plain but comfortable modern hotel with spacious and well-equipped rooms; also has a pleasant roof terrace.

📍 F11 ✉ 533 Thanon Silom ☎ /fax 234 4051 🚌 A/C bus 2, 4, 5, 15

TRINITY CITY

Tastefully decorated hotel with excellent rooms, very friendly staff, and even a small swimming pool and fitness centre on the roof.

📍 G11 ✉ 425 Soi Silom 5 ☎ 231 5050; fax 231 5417 🚌 A/C bus 2, 4, 5, 15

A comfortable YMCA

Many travellers recommend the YMCA Collins International House (✉ 27 Thanon Satorn Tai ☎ 287 2727; fax 287 1966) for its central location and spotless rooms. It also boasts a pool, gym and some good-value restaurants. The YWCA is at 13 Thanon Satorn Tai (☎ 286 1936; fax 287 3016).

BUDGET HOTELS

Thanon Khao San

First came backpackers in search of the pleasures of the Orient, then local Thais and Chinese who saw the possibilities... Thanon Khao San and its neighbourhood is now *the* place for cheap beds, cheap eats, cheap clothes and cheap beer. If you're on a tight budget, this is the place to be, but arrive early in the day if you want to find a bed. One thing's for sure, wherever you stay it's going to be lively.

BANGKOK CHRISTIAN GUESTHOUSE

Lovely guesthouse with wonderful staff, simple but very tidy rooms and a great lawn with a fish pond. As the name suggests, there is a Christian atmosphere. Usually fully booked a few weeks in advance.
✚ G11 ✉ 123 Soi Sala Daeng 2, off Thanon Convent ☎ 233 6303 🚍 A/C bus 2, 4, 5, 15

CHAI'S HOUSE

Better-than-average Khao San hotel with perfectly clean rooms, some with balconies overgrown with bougainvillaea. Very homely atmosphere and an average restaurant.
✚ C7 ✉ 49/4–8 Chao Fa Soi Rongmai, Khao San ☎ 281 4901; fax 281 8686 🚍 A/C bus 3, 6, 9, 12, 39, 44

CHAO PHRAYA RIVERSIDE

Clean rooms with excellent views of the river in an old-style Chinese house set in the heart of Chinatown. The service can be abrupt but the location in great.
✚ D9/10 ✉ 1128 Thanon Song Wat, opposite the Chinese school ☎ 222 6344; fax 223 1696 🚍 A/C bus 1, 7 ⛴ Ratchawong pier

DYNASTY INN

Small but friendly hotel with well-maintained rooms.
✚ J9 ✉ 5/4–5 Sukhumwit Soi 4 ☎ 252 4522; fax 255 1111 🚍 A/C bus 1, 8, 11, 13

GOLDEN PALACE

Slightly faded hotel popular with middle-class tourists on a budget. Has clean rooms and a swimming pool.
✚ J9 ✉ 15 Soi Ruam Ruedi, off Thanon Ploenchit ☎ 252 5115/6 🚍 A/C bus 1, 8, 11, 13

LEK GUEST HOUSE

Basic but clean rooms, some with balconies, and a roof terrace. Rooms on the street side are noisy. Very cheap.
✚ C7 ✉ 125 Thanon Khao San, Banglamphoo ☎ 281 2775 🚍 A/C bus 6, 11, 17

MALAYSIA HOTEL

The backpackers' hotel *par excellence*. A large noticeboard is covered with advice from knowing travellers, and the atmosphere is very laid-back. Swimming pool.
✚ H11 ✉ 54 Soi Ngam Duphli, off Thanon Rama IV ☎ 286 3582; fax 249 3120 🚍 A/C bus 7

RIVER VIEW GUEST HOUSE

Highly recommended budget hotel, with spacious rooms overlooking the Chao Phraya. An excellent breakfast of cereal and fresh fruit is served on the top floor. Book in advance.
✚ E10 ✉ 768 Soi Phanu Rangsee, Thanon Song Wat ☎ 234 5429; fax 237 5771 ⛴ Krom Choha pier

SALATHAI

Family-run guest-house with clean and pleasant rooms, some furnished with bamboo furniture. Shared bathrooms. Excellent value for money.
✚ J12 ✉ 15 Soi Sri Bomphen, off Thanon Rama IV ☎ 287 1436 🚍 A/C bus 2, 4, 5, 15

BANGKOK
travel facts

ARRIVING & DEPARTING

Before you go

- Visitors must hold a valid passport and proof of onward passage.
- Nationals of the UK, USA, Ireland, Australia, Canada, New Zealand and most other European countries can stay in Thailand for 30 days without a visa. Other nationals can get a 30-day visa at Bangkok International Airport. Visa-free entry *cannot* be extended, so if you want to stay longer than 30 days, apply before entry for a 60-day tourist visa.
- Extensions and re-entry visas can be obtained from ✉ Section 3, Old Building, Immigration Bureau, Soi Suan Phlu, Thanon Satorn Tai ☎ 287 3101/10.
- Non-immigrant visas for 90 days are issued to business travellers.
- No vaccinations are required.

Climate

- Mar–May is the hot season, with temperatures up to 38°C (100°F) and humidity up to 90 per cent.
- Jun/Jul–Oct is the rainy season, with average temperatures of 29°C (84°F).
- Nov–Feb is pleasant and cool, with average temperatures of 26°C (79°F) and lower humidity.

Arriving by air

- Bangkok International Airport is 22km north of the city centre.
- Public taxis have meters and wait at the taxi rank outside the airport. Beware of unlicensed taxis, which often overcharge. Minivans and limousines can be booked (and pre-paid) at the Thai Airways Limousine desk, counter 7, which also issues tickets for the Airport Express Train. The latter runs 5–6 times daily – a shuttle bus connects the airport terminal with Don Muang Station, from where trains run to Hua Lamphong Station. To reach riverside hotels during rush hour take the Airport River Express (700B), which cuts the journey time to under 1½ hours (book in advance through hotel reservation offices). An A/C bus service connects the airport to Thanon Silom, Sanam Luang and Phra Khanong every 15 minutes 5AM–11PM.

Arriving by train

- Malaysia and Singapore trains arrive at Hua Lamphong Station.

Customs regulations

- Licences are required to export antiques, art objects and religious articles (➤ 70, panel). No more than 50,000B may be exported.

Departure/airport tax

- 30B for domestic flights and 250B for international flights.

ESSENTIAL FACTS

Travel insurance

- Travel insurance covering medical expenses is a must.
- Keep all your receipts in order to claim on your return home.

Opening hours

- Offices: Mon–Fri 8:30–12, 1–4:30.
- Banks: Mon–Fri 10–4.
- Bangkok Bank and exchange counters: Mon–Sun 7AM–8PM.
- Shops: Mon–Sun 10–6:30 or 7; smaller shops often stay open 12 hours a day.

National holidays

- Some holidays are calculated according to the lunar calendar and vary from year to year.
- New Year (31 Dec, 1 Jan).
- Chinese New Year (early Feb).
- Maga Puja (full moon; mid-Feb).

- Chakri Day (6 Apr).
- Songkran (Thai New Year; 12–14 Apr).
- Royal Ploughing Ceremony (early May).
- Coronation Day (5 May).
- Visaka Puja (full moon; May).
- Asalha Puja (full moon; Jul).
- HM Queen Sirikit's Birthday; Mother's Day (12 Aug).
- Ok Pansa (late Oct).
- Chulalongkorn Day (23 Oct).
- Loy Krathong (early Nov).
- HM King Bhumibol's Birthday; Father's Day (5 Dec).
- Constitution Day (10 Dec).

Money matters

- The currency is baht (B), divided in 100 satang. The coins are 25 and 50 satang, 1 baht, 5 baht and 10 baht. Notes are 20, 50, 100, 500 and 1,000 baht.
- Most hotels, restaurants and larger shops accept major credit cards, although some add a surcharge.
- Traveller's cheques get a slightly better exchange rate than cash.
- You can withdraw Thai baht with credit cards from cash machines.

Electricity

- 220V, 50-cycle AC. Most hotels have 110V shaver outlets.

Tourist offices
Overseas offices

- Australia ✉ Level 2, National Australia Bank House, 255 George Street, Sydney, NSW 2000 ☎ 9247 7549; fax 9251 2465.
- UK ✉ 49 Albemarle Street, London W1X 3FE ☎ 0839 300 800 (charged at premium rate); fax 0171 629 5519.
- USA ✉ 5 World Trade Center, Suite 3443, New York, NY10048 ☎ 212/432 0433; fax 212/912 0920. ✉ 3440 Wilshire Boulevard, Suite 1100, Los Angeles, CA90010 ☎ 213/382 2353; fax 213/389 7544. ✉ 303 East Wacker Drive, Suite 400, Chicago IL60601 ☎ 312 819 3990; fax 312 565 0359.

Main local tourist information centres

- ✉ Counter at Bangkok International Airport ☎ 523 8972 🕐 Daily 8:30–4:30.
- ✉ 372 Thanon Bamrung Muang, east of the Grand Palace ☎ 226 0060/226 0085 🕐 Daily 8:30–4:30.
- ✉ 1 Thanon Naphralarn ☎ 226 0056 🕐 Daily 8:30–4:30.
- Some Tourism Authority of Thailand (TAT) information is now available on the worldwide web at website http://www.cs.ait. ac.th/tat/. E-mail enquiries can be sent to TAT at the following address: tat@cs.ait.ac.th.

Student travellers

- Museums offer a 50 per cent discount to holders of an International Student Identity Card.

Etiquette

- Thais show great respect for their royal family and religious personalities, as should visitors. Monks are forbidden to touch women and cannot receive offerings directly from them. All Buddha images are sacred.
- A public display of anger is taboo.
- Cover arms and legs in temples.
- It is insulting to touch someone's head or back, and it is rude to point toes or the soles of feet at someone or at a Buddha image. Remove shoes upon entering a temple or a private home.
- Thais rarely shake hands, instead placing them together under their chin in a *wai*.

Women travellers

- Thailand is generally safe for single women travellers, but recent social changes have brought an end to many traditions and it pays to be aware of potential dangers.

Visitors with disabilities

- Bangkok is particularly difficult for visitors with disabilities – pavements are uneven, roads busy with traffic and the river boats hardly stop long enough for anyone to jump on. For information call Disabled People's International Thailand ☎ 255 1718; fax 252 3678.

Places of worship

- Anglican: Christ Church ✉ 11 Thanon Convent, between Thanon Silom and Thanon Satorn Nuea ☎ 234 3634. International Church ✉ 67 Sukhumwit Soi 19 ☎ 253 2205.
- Catholic: Assumption Cathedral ✉ 23 Soi Oriental, near the Oriental Hotel ☎ 234 8556.
- Jewish: Jewish Association of Thailand ✉ Soi Sai Pan 2, off Sukhumwit Soi 22 ☎ 258 2195.
- Muslim: Haroon Mosque ✉ Thanon Charoen Krung (New Road), near the post office.

Time differences

- Bangkok is 7 hours ahead of GMT. In winter: UK -7 hours, Europe -6, New York -12, Australia +3, New Zealand +5. In summer: add 1 hour to the above.

Toilets

- Most hotels and restaurants have Western-style toilets, while *wats*, shops and some budget hotels may have an Asian-style hole in the ground.

PUBLIC TRANSPORT

Buses

- Public buses are cheap but get extremely crowded and are popular with pickpockets.
- With Bangkok's notorious heat and traffic it may be worth paying for an air-conditioned public bus (indicated as 'A/C bus' in this guide). Services stop at 11PM, although a few night buses run, including the No 2 from Sanam Luang to Thanon Sukhumwit.
- The red air-conditioned Microbuses cost 30B.

Riverbuses

- The Chao Phraya River Express Company's boats ☎ 222 5330 serve piers (*tha*) on both sides of the river, are fast and enjoyable, avoid traffic jams and are inexpensive (5–10B). Boats run about every 10 minutes daily 6–6.
- Next to express boat piers are piers for smaller cross-river ferries. These cost 1B and also run about every 10 minutes daily 6–6.
- Public long-tail boats (5–10B) leave for Thonburi from Ratchawong, Tian, Chang Wang Luang and Maha Rat when full.
- The main express boat piers are marked on the fold-out map.

Where to get maps

- Bangkok bookshops and the main TAT office sell the *Latest Tour Guide to Bangkok & Thailand*, called the 'Bangkok Bus Map'.
- Other good maps include *Bangkok's Best* by Aaron Frankel, and Nancy Chandler's *Map of Bangkok*.

Taxis

- The fastest and cheapest taxis are motorbike taxis. These have no meters, so haggling is necessary before setting off.
- *Tuk tuks* are motorised open-fronted three-wheelers. They carry up to three passengers, are slightly more expensive and expose passengers to Bangkok's worst pollution. Discuss the price in advance.
- Most taxi-cabs are now metered (known as taxi meter) and are also

air-conditioned. A 24-hour phone-a-cab service is available for 10B extra above the metered fare ☎ 319 9911. Insist that the meter is switched on as soon as you leave (the flagfare is 35B) and add extra if you use a tollway.

MEDIA & COMMUNICATIONS

Telephones

- Local calls from red or silver public pay phones cost 1B for three minutes. Most hotel lobbies, restaurants and shops have public pay phones that take 5B coins.
- International calls are cheapest from the main Telephone Office, in the same building as the GPO (see below), open 24 hours. Hotels always add a surcharge.
- From 6 to 10PM there is a 50 per cent discount on international calls; from 10PM to 7AM it is 67 per cent. For information, dial 13.
- Faxes can be sent from the Telephone and Telegraph Office at the GPO ⊙ 24 hours, or from fax bureaux and most hotels.

Post offices

- The General Post Office (GPO) is at ☎ Thanon Charoen Krung (New Road), between the Oriental and Sheraton hotels ⊙ Mon–Fri 8–8; Sat–Sun and holidays 8–1.
- Stamps for airmail letters under 5g to Europe, Australia and USA cost 15B; those for postcards cost 10B.

Newspapers and magazines

- The two local English-language daily newspapers, the *Bangkok Post* and the *Nation*, cover Thai politics, international news and local cultural events.
- The *International Herald Tribune* and the *Asian Wall Street Journal* are available on the day of publication, Mon–Fri.

- The monthly magazines *Where?* and *Look East*, complimentary in hotel rooms, cover features and events in Bangkok. *Metro* magazine, also a monthly publication and available from bookshops, has excellent listings for all cultural events.

International newsagents

- Most five-star hotels have newsstands selling the major international papers.
- Bookshops such as Asia Books ✉ Ground and 3rd floors of the Landmark Plaza, Sukhumwit Soi 4 ☎ 253 9786 and The Bookseller Co ✉ 81 Thanon Patpong 1 ☎ 233 1717 also offer newspapers and magazines.

Radio and television

- Radio Thailand at 97FM has a daily English-language programme from 6AM to midnight. The BBC World Service and the Voice of America can be picked up on short wave. (Check schedules before leaving home.)
- Cable TV with international channels is available at up-market hotels. For broadcast TV, check the television pages of the *Nation* or the *Bangkok Post*.

EMERGENCIES

Sensible precautions

- Bangkok is generally a safe city, but pickpockets and bag-snatchers do operate in crowded places, especially on buses, river express boats and ferries.
- Leave money and important documents in your hotel's safe-deposit box if possible, and never carry traveller's cheques together with a list of their numbers.
- Take care of credit cards. Keep all receipts and destroy carbons.

- Beware of 'bargain' gems, jewellery or other objects, which might later prove to be worthless. Also beware of getting involved in a game of Thai cards as you are sure to lose.
- Beware of taking someone to your room, or of accepting food or drink from strangers, as you may be drugged and robbed.
- Thais are serious about wanting to stop drug smuggling. Border security is efficient and the maximum penalty is death.

Lost property

- If you are robbed, call the tourist police Crime Suppression Division immediately ☎ 225 7758 ext 4.

Medical treatment

- All listed hospitals have 24-hour emergency services, but you may need your passport and a deposit of 20,000B. Your medical insurance policy may not be accepted, although major credit cards are.
- Private hospitals: Bangkok Nursing Home ✉ 9 Thanon Convent, between Thanon Silom and Thanon Satorn Nuea ☎ 233 2610; Bumrungat Medical Centre/Hospital ✉ 33 Sukhumwit Soi 3 ☎ 253 0259.
- Public hospitals: Bangkok General Hospital ✉ 2 Soi Soonvijai 7, Thanon Phetburi ☎ 318 0066; Chulalongkorn Hospital ✉ Thanon Rama IV ☎ 252 8181.
- Contact your hotel reception first in case of a medical emergency.
- Keep all receipts for claiming on your travel insurance when you return home.

Medicines

- British Dispensary ✉ Near Soi 5, 109 Thanon Sukhumwit ☎ 252 8056, or ✉ Corner of Soi Oriental and Thanon Charoen Krung (New Road) ☎ 234 0174.
- Phuket Dispensary ✉ Near Soi 21, 383 Thanon Sukhumwit ☎ 252 9179.
- Thai pharmacies are generally well stocked, and many drugs are available over the counter.
- Pharmacies are open daily 8AM–9PM in most places, but there is no all-night service. In an emergency, contact a hospital.

Emergency phone numbers

- Ambulance ☎ 252 2171/5.
- Fire ☎ 199.
- Police ☎ 191.
- Tourist police ☎ 1699 or 652 1721.

Embassies and consulates

- Australia ✉ 37 Thanon Satorn Tai ☎ 287 2680.
- Canada ✉ 11th and 12th floors, Boonmiter Building, 138 Thanon Silom ☎ 238 4452.
- France ✉ 35 Soi Rongpasi Kao (Customs House Lane), Thanon Charoen Krung (New Road) ☎ 266 8250; consular section (visas) ✉ 29 Thanon Satorn Tai ☎ 285 6104.
- Germany ✉ 9 Thanon Satorn Tai ☎ 213 2331/6.
- Italy ✉ 399 Thanon Nang Linchi ☎ 285 4090/3.
- New Zealand ✉ 93 Thanon Witthayu (Wireless Road) ☎ 251 8165.
- UK ✉ 1031 Thanon Ploenchit ☎ 253 0191.
- USA ✉ 95 Thanon Witthayu (Wireless Road) ☎ 252 5040.

LANGUAGE

- Although English is widely spoken in hotels and restaurants, it is useful to have some notion of Thai. The Thai language is quite difficult to master as one syllable can be pronounced in five tones, each of which will carry a different meaning. The classic example of this is the syllable *mai* which, in the different tones, can mean 'new', 'wood', 'burnt', 'not?'. and 'not'. So *Mái mài mâi mâi mäi* means: 'New wood doesn't burn, does it?' Tricky, *mâi*? As if this wasn't enough, consonants are pronounced slightly differently. Ask a Thai to pronounce the words listed below for you in the right tone. And for taxi- and *tuk tuk*-drivers, notorious for misunderstanding addresses, ask someone to write down your destination in Thai.

Greetings

hello sawat-dii khrap (man), sawat-dii kha (woman)
how are you? pen yangai?
I'm fine sabaay dii
thank you khawp khun
goodbye laa gorn
see you later phop gan mai
sorry, excuse me kor toh
what is your name? khun cheu arai?
my name is... (man) phom cheu...
my name is... (woman) diichan cheu...
(I) don't understand mai khao jai
it doesn't matter mai pen rai
yes chai
no mai chai

Getting around

where is...? ...yu thii nai?
how do I get to...? pai...yung ngai?
turn right lii-o kwaa
turn left lii-o sai
straight ahead dtrong dtrong

Shopping

how much? thao rai?
cheap thuuk
too expensive phaeng pai

Numbers

0	suun	**8**	paet
1	neung	**9**	kao
2	sawng	**10**	sip
3	sahm	**11**	sip-et
4	sii	**12**	sip-sawng
5	haa	**20**	yii-sip
6	hok	**30**	sahm-sip
7	jet	**100**	neung roy

Time

today wan nii
tomorrow phrung nii
yesterday meua waan

Glossary

baht **Thai currency**
baan **house, village**
bot **main chapel of a temple**
chakri **military commander**
chedi **pagoda, where relics are kept**
farang **foreigner**
hawng suam **toilet**
klong **canal**
mae, mae nam, lak nam **river**
nakhon, muang, thanii **city**
nao **cold**
pak nam **river mouth**
prang **tower**
raan aahaa **restaurant**
rakang **bell**
rawn **hot**
reua hang yao **long-tail boat**
rim nam **river bank**
rohng raem **hotel**
rot fai **train**
rot maw-toe-sa **motorcycle**
rot meh, rot bat **bus**
rot yon **taxi**
sanaam bin **airport**
sathaanii **station**
soi **lane**
talaat **market**
tha **pier, harbour**
thanon **street, road**
tuk tuk **motorised rickshaw**
viharn **hall for religious ritual**
wai **Thai greeting**
wat **temple, monastery**

INDEX

CityPack
Bangkok

Written by   Anthony Sattin and Sylvie Franquet
Edited, designed and produced by
AA Publishing

Maps   © The Automobile Association 1997, 1999
Fold-out map © RV Reise- und Verkehrsverlag Munich · Stuttgart
© Cartography: GeoData

Distributed in the United Kingdom by AA Publishing, Norfolk House, Priestley Road,
Basingstoke, Hampshire, RG24 9NY.

The contents of this publication are believed correct at the time of printing. Nevertheless, the
publishers cannot be held responsible for any errors or omissions or for changes in the details
given in this guide or for the consequences of any reliance on the information provided by the
same. Assessments of attractions, hotels, restaurants and so forth are based upon the author's
own personal experience and, therefore, descriptions given in this guide necessarily contain an
element of subjective opinion which may not reflect the publishers' opinion or dictate a
reader's own experiences on another occasion.
We have tried to ensure accuracy in this guide, but things do change and we would be grateful
if readers would advise us of any inaccuracies they may encounter.

ISBN 0 7495 1894 4

Published by AA Publishing (a trading name of Automobile Association Developments
Limited, whose registered office is Norfolk House, Priestley Road, Basingstoke, Hampshire
RG24 9NY. Registered number 1878835).

Colour separation by Daylight Colour Art Pte Ltd, Singapore
Printed and bound by Dai Nippon Printing Co (Hong Kong) Ltd.

Acknowledgements
The Automobile Association wishes to thank the following library for its assistance in
the preparation of this book: Eye Ubiquitous 47; Spectrum Colour Library 40a, 46a, 46b,
58. The remaining photographs are held in the Association's own library (AA Photo
Library) and were taken by Jim Holmes, with the exception of pages 5a, 5b, 7, 8, 9a, 9b,
12, 13a, 14, 16, 17, 19, 20, 21, 23, 25a, 25b, 27b, 28, 30a, 30b, 31, 32, 33a, 35a, 35b, 36a,
36b, 37, 40b, 41a, 42, 43a, 43b, 44b, 45a, 45b, 49a, 49b, 50, 52, 55, 56, 60a, 60b, 61a, 61b,
87a, 87b which were taken by Rick Strange.

Cover photographs
Main picture: Pictor International – London Insets: AA Photo Library (Rick Strange)

ORIGINAL COPY EDITOR *Susi Bailey* INDEXER *Marie Lorimer*
REVISION VERIFIERS *Anthony Sattin and Sylvie Franquet*
SECOND EDITION UPDATED BY *OutHouse Publishing Service*

Titles in the CityPack series

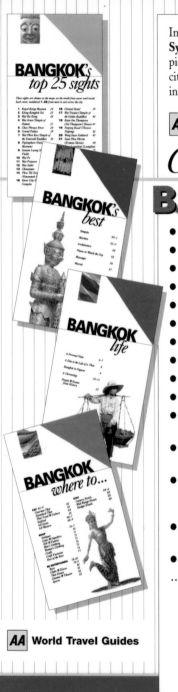

BANGKOK's
top 25 sights

BANGKOK's
best

BANGKOK
life

BANGKOK
where to...

AA World Travel Guides

In **CityPack BANGKOK**
Sylvie Franquet and **Anthony Sattin**
pick out the best of everything the
city has to offer – whatever your
interests, taste and budget.

AA

CityPack
BANGKOK

- Top 25 Sights
- Itineraries
- Walks & Evening Strolls
- Organised Sightseeing
- Excursions
- Temples
- Markets
- Architecture
- Places to Watch the City
- Massages
- Restaurants – Thai, Seafood,
  all Asian, Western
- Antiques, Gems & Jewellery,
  Silk & Fabrics, Crafts
- Bars, Clubs & Discos, Thai
  Dance, Cinema & Theatre,
  Sports
- Hotels – Luxury, Mid-Range,
  Budget
- Detailed Practical Information

… and much more

ISBN 0-7495-1894-4

9 780749 518943

£6.99